THE MOBI
DESIGN JOURNEY

The Mobile Course Design Journey provides practical strategies to college and university educators and faculty support professionals looking to develop accessible mobile learning experiences. Given the near-ubiquity of mobile device ownership today, creating courses that can be completed entirely on a mobile device is essential to captivating student attention and supporting equity-minded pedagogy. This book frames effective mobile design within a continuum in which educators can make gradual yet meaningful changes to their instruction and course content while leveraging learners' existing tools and literacies. Original, ready-to-use features such as a rubric for evaluating the mobile-friendliness of course content and assignments as well as a toolkit for leading workshops on mobile design will further help to demystify mobile learning in higher education.

Alex Rockey is Professor of Academic Technology at Bakersfield College, USA.

THE MOBILE COURSE DESIGN JOURNEY

Transforming Access in Higher Education

Alex Rockey

NEW YORK AND LONDON

Designed cover image: © shutterstock

First published 2024
by Routledge
605 Third Avenue, New York, NY 10158

and by Routledge
4 Park Square, Milton Park, Abingdon, Oxon, OX14 4RN

Routledge is an imprint of the Taylor & Francis Group, an informa business

Library of Congress Cataloging-in-Publication Data
Names: Rockey, Alex, author.
Title: The mobile course design journey : transforming access in higher education / Alex Rockey.
Description: New York, NY : Routledge, 2024. | Includes bibliographical references and index. |
Identifiers: LCCN 2023019986 (print) | LCCN 2023019987 (ebook) | ISBN 9781032358253 (hardback) | ISBN 9781032354217 (paperback) | ISBN 9781003328773 (ebook)
Subjects: LCSH: Mobile communication systems in education. | Education, Higher--Web-based instruction. | Educational change. | Education, Higher--Effect of technological innovations on.
Classification: LCC LB1044.84 .R57 2024 (print) | LCC LB1044.84 (ebook) | DCC 378.1/7--dc23/eng/20230526
LC record available at https://lccn.loc.gov/2023019986
LC ebook record available at https://lccn.loc.gov/2023019987

ISBN: 978-1-032-35825-3 (hbk)
ISBN: 978-1-032-35421-7 (pbk)
ISBN: 978-1-003-32877-3 (ebk)

DOI: 10.4324/9781003328773

Typeset in Joanna
by MPS Limited, Dehradun

For Hylia – I'm so lucky to be your mom.

CONTENTS

ACKNOWLEDGEMENTS

Over the past year, I have had many dreams about this book. They are mostly long, boring dreams in which I slowly talk about the research I have been reading. But this book has been brewing in my mind for much longer than a year and wouldn't have been possible without the support of my friends, family, and colleagues.

Sonya Christian, Michelle Pacansky-Brock, and Jenae Cohn, I am beyond humbled you agreed to read my manuscript. Sonya, your leadership inspires innovation. Your support of my work in mobile-friendly design gave me the courage and confidence to tackle this book. Thank you. Michelle, thank you for taking the time to meet with me when I was a grad student for an informational interview. The kindness you showed in answering my questions has meant so much to me. Jenae, thank you for guidance and support as I have worked on this project.

Thank you to the California Educational Learning Lab for funding "Access for Equity" and creating an opportunity for our team to build a mobile-friendly course and contribute to research on how and why students are using phones for learning. Thank you to Rob Rubalcaba, Fabiola Torres, Samantha Eastman, Margaret Merrill, Mindy Colin, and Jenae Cohn for walking down this road with me for our students.

Bill Moseley, Dana Ferris, Rebekka Andersen, Carl Whithaus, and Andy Jones, thank you for your mentorship and for teaching me how to be a scholar. Your patience and knowledge continue to support and propel me today. Bill, thank you for creating an atmosphere of innovation and for encouraging me to pursue the idea of mobile-friendly course design. Andy, thank you for teaching me so much about writing and for helping me find my love of academic technology. I am so blessed to have gotten to work with all of you.

Thank you to my parents, my aunt Stephanie, my cousin Barb and aunt Lisha, and my grandmother Montine. Mom, thank you for telling me the stories of our family and for helping me on every step of my educational journey. Thank you for walking with me all day on the Madison campus in the August muggy heat so I knew how to get to my classes. Dad, thank you for teaching me imaginary numbers when I was in third grade, and thank you for teaching me how to use coffee beans to understand math. Stephanie, thank you for being my pen pal growing up and for teaching me about writing at an early age. Barb and Lisha, thank you so much for your enthusiasm for this book. Montine, you passed away when I was two, but I think of you often. Thank you for instilling in my mom a dedication to education and a passion for life. Your values guide us today.

My husband, William Rockey. Thank you for showing strength through patience. And listening so intently to every single thought I have. As Hylia said, "I can't pick one thing to say about you, because you are so many things to me." So I'll simply say thank you for building this life with me and for your love.

Finally, thank you to my daughter Hylia Rockey. I can't believe I get to be your mom. You are the kindest, smartest, strongest person I know. I applied to grad school when I was pregnant with you, and ever since we have been on this journey together. Thank you for your unabashed enthusiasm for my work. I loved reading Chapter 12 to you while we cuddled on the couch. I loved when you said: "I love my mommy so much. She is amazing, and I am inspired by her." Hylia, I love you so much. You are amazing, and I am inspired by you.

PART 1

WHY DOES MOBILE DESIGN MATTER?

1

CONSIDER OUR LEARNERS

DESIGNING FOR USE AND REDUCING BARRIERS OF ACCESS

Beginning the mobile-design journey

What is the first thing you look at when you wake up in the morning? Most mornings, I'm embarrassed to admit, the first thing I look at is my phone. And I'm not alone. Surveys on mobile device usage have created some headline-worthy findings, including:

- "71% of Americans say they check their phones within the first 10 minutes of waking up
- 74% of Americans feel uneasy leaving their phone at home
- 70% of Americans check their phones within five minutes of receiving a notification" (Wheelwright, 2022)

Despite widespread smartphone usage, courses are typically not designed to leverage mobile devices for learning. The smartphones learners carry with them everywhere are relegated to be used only for social media and

DOI: 10.4324/9781003328773-2

games. Without leveraging mobile devices for learning, smartphones become more like an expensive deck of cards that can take pictures than a tool that has the power to transform access to high-quality educational opportunities. To fully serve learners in the 21st century, we as educators must embark on a journey of mobile design. We must explore ways in which we can design courses that provide opportunities for students to use their phones for learning.

Mobile design: An approach to universal design for learning

Mobile-friendly course design is an approach to universal design for learning (UDL) that acknowledges learners are frequently on their phones and that not all learners have access to reliable, high-speed internet. UDL provides a framework to guide educators in designing a course that can be individualized to serve a diverse group of learners (CAST, 2018). Educators can use UDL principles to create a course that can be easily customized and individualized for learners. The goal of UDL is to "change the design of the environment rather than to change the learner" (CAST, 2018). Using a UDL approach allows educators to make their course accessible to all learners before the course begins without having to scramble to accommodate individual learners once the semester has already started.

UDL principles help educators serve all learners. For example, accurately captioned videos benefit learners who may be hard of hearing, but they also benefit learners who may be watching videos in a noisy environment or who may appreciate the opportunity to see the words. Just as UDL benefits learners, it also makes an instructor's job easier as there are less last-minute adaptations to a course to provide accommodations to learners on an individual basis.

Mobile design aligns with UDL principles. When we follow mobile-design principles, we can create a course for which learners can use their phones. In fully mobile-friendly courses, learners can use their phones exclusively, but they can also move fluidly between their phones and computers to make progress on their courses. And, of course, learners could still choose to use only a computer or laptop to complete their coursework. By integrating mobile-design principles, we can create courses in which learners can use their phones as much or as little as they want to, but we can also create a course that benefits all learners. Many of the mobile-design principles can help learners who are using computers. For example, when we chunk content into smaller pieces it helps learners who are relying on the small screen of their phone to complete coursework, but it also helps all learners as it lessens the cognitive load and helps learners to focus on what they need to learn from each chunk of content.

By designing courses that learners can complete on their mobile device, we are leveraging UDL principles to create a learning experience that adapts to meet student needs. Mobile-friendly course design is not an either/or, but rather a journey in which we can constantly iterate and reflect to make our courses easier to use on mobile devices. As with every journey, we can start with just a few steps that can make a big difference to our students. To embark on this journey, we first need to understand why mobile design helps to create courses that align with how students use technology and reduce barriers to learning.

The why of mobile design

As educators, there are two major reasons we should consider mobile design. First, mobile design provides the opportunity to align our courses with how students already use their mobile devices in their day-to-day lives. Second, mobile design reduces barriers of access learners may experience with a lack of home internet and/or the multiple demands on learners' time. The following sections explore in more detail how mobile-friendly courses can serve learners by aligning with student use of smartphones and reducing barriers of access.

Designing for use

How much time would you guess students spend on their phones each day? I posed this question during a keynote my colleagues and I were giving on mobile learning. The chat in Zoom blew up with faculty guesses of "five hours," "12 hours," and "24/7." Many faculty guessed "constantly."

Research on actual usage suggests that students can spend about four to five hours a day on their mobile devices alone (Andrews et al., 2015; Felisoni & Godoi, 2018). One study found that students actually spent over five hours a day on their phones and used their phones on average about 85 times a day (Andrews et al., 2015). Another study found that students spent an average of 230 minutes a day, or almost four hours, on their cell phones (Felisoni & Godoi, 2018). Although it's helpful to consider how much time students spend on their phones a day, the concept of "digital tethering" (Savin-Badin, 2015, p. 1) moves beyond a focus on minutes and hours and helps to paint a picture of how deeply connected and reliant students are on their phones.

Savin-Badin defines *digital tethering* as "the constant interaction and engagement with digital technology, the sense of being 'always on', 'always engaged', characterized by wearing a mobile device, texting at dinner, or driving illegally while 'Facebooking'" (2015, p. 1). The concept of digital tethering puts a name to the pull many of us feel from our mobile devices. For many of us, including our students, our phones are more than something that we check or use throughout the day. Phones become an integral part of our day. They sleep next to us at night, they wake us up in the morning, they help us find our way, and they tell us what our friends and family are doing. They may even tell us when to go to bed.

Although students frequently use their phones for personal purposes, they rarely use their mobile devices for learning (Kirschner & De Bruyckere, 2017). It's no surprise as courses are often designed to be completed on a computer. When we design courses for computers without consideration of the experience on mobile devices, it can often augment the limitations of phones without realizing the benefits. Research suggests common limitations of mobile devices include:

- attention pulling (Barden & Bygroves, 2018),
- small screens (Eschenbrenner & Nah, 2019), and
- negative perceptions of mobile device usage for learning (Ally, 2013; Barden & Bygroves, 2018).

However, there are also benefits to mobile devices, including:

- anytime/anywhere learning (Ally, 2013; Barden & Bygroves, 2018),
- portability (Attenborough & Abbott, 2018; Kobus et al., 2013),
- convenience (Barden & Bygroves, 2018),
- multimodal capabilities (Cochrane & Bateman, 2010), and
- connection (Cochrane & Bateman, 2010; Cross, 2019; Danish & Hmelo-Silver, 2020; Nasser, 2014).

Mobile devices, like any technology, are not neutral. If we do not strategically work to minimize their limitations and maximize their benefits, we can inadvertently maximize their limitations without realizing their benefits. For example, if we don't manage the pull of our mobile devices, we could be distracted from playing with our kids to check a notification from Instagram. We could also be distracted while we're driving by a notification from Facebook or Twitter.

Similarly, when we don't intentionally design for mobile devices in our courses, we can maximize the limitations of mobile devices. Learners can be distracted by notifications in our classes and decide to check their social media accounts instead of participating in a group discussion. Learners can also be frustrated by the endless scroll on a page in the Learning Management System (LMS) and stop reading an assignment on their phone. As educators, designing mobile-friendly courses allows us to maximize the potential benefits of mobile devices, like anytime/anywhere learning (Ally, 2013; Barden & Bygroves, 2018), and minimize the limitations of a small screen (Eschenbrenner & Nah, 2019).

Though we often design courses to be accessed on computers, learners often access our courses via their phones (Baldwin & Ching, 2020; Wilcox et al., 2016). If a course is not designed to maximize the benefits of smartphones for learning, it can be a clunky and frustrating experience. Learners may quickly get frustrated with having to endlessly scroll to read a page. Learners may even just stop an activity if it is not easy to complete on a phone. Although learners may later return to the activity when (and if) they have access to a computer and the internet, we are missing an opportunity to redirect learner attention from social media to our courses when we don't design mobile-friendly courses.

When we design our courses to align with how learners use mobile devices for personal purposes, we can capture student attention for our courses. Capturing a bit of this attention for our courses can make a substantial difference in how we support student learning. Imagine if a learner is scrolling through TikTok but receives a message from their instructor to encourage them to complete their assignment that is due tomorrow. And imagine if that assignment could be completed on their phone. By redirecting attention to our courses, we can make our class move beyond the confines of walls or even the confines of a laptop.

Designing mobile-friendly courses can also prepare learners for ways they will need to leverage their phones in their future careers. Although students often use mobile devices for personal purposes, they have less experience using their phones for learning (Kirschner & De Bruyckere, 2017). This is problematic as students will likely need to use their phones in their future careers (Harris & Greer, 2021; Narayan et al., 2019). Whether they use their phones to communicate with colleagues on platforms like Slack or Teams or to amplify work on social media platforms, effective use of smartphones is increasingly an important 21st-century career skill. By creating space for learners to use their phones to both access course content and create assignments, we can provide learners space to play and explore ways in which they can use their phones to help prepare them for future careers.

Mobile devices are not neutral tools, but when we align the design of our courses with how learners already use mobile devices in their personal lives, we can captivate student attention towards our courses and prepare learners for 21st-century careers. By designing mobile-friendly courses, we can leverage the benefits of mobile devices and minimize the limitations to support student learning with a tool that students use frequently throughout the day.

Reducing barriers of access

Mobile design can also support equity by transforming access to higher education for:

- students without home internet,
- students in emerging economies,
- so-called nontraditional students, and
- students experiencing disruptions.

By designing mobile-friendly courses, we can leverage phones to remove barriers of access to high-quality educational opportunities for students across the world.

Creating access regardless of home internet

About 15% of adults in the United States use their smartphones to access the internet as they do not have home internet (Pew Research Center, 2021). Smartphone dependency varies by age, income, and ethnicity. For adults ages 18–29, there is a trend towards increased smartphone dependency (Pew Research Center, 2021). In the year 2021, 28% of 18- to 29-year-olds relied on their phones to access the internet (Pew Research Center, 2021). Smartphone dependency also varies based on income. Lower income households rely on their phones to access the internet. For households earning less than $30,000, 27% were dependent on their phones for internet access (Pew Research Center, 2021). Nineteen percent of households earning between $30,000 and $49,000 did not have access to home internet (Pew Research Center, 2021). In contrast, only 6% of households earning over $75,000 a year did not have home internet (Pew Research Center, 2021). As we consider income and its correlation with smartphone dependency, it is important to remember the median income in 2020 was $41,535 in the United States (Shrider et al., 2021). Finally, access to home internet varies based on ethnicity. In 2021, 25% of Hispanic adults, 17% of black adults, and 12% of white adults, respectively, relied on their mobile devices to access the internet at home (Pew Research Center, 2021).

Although inequities in home internet access existed before COVID-19 (Pew Research Center, 2019a), emergency moves to remote teaching highlighted these inequities and presented challenges for learners trying to continue their education despite campus closures. Many colleges and schools across the country realized access to home internet was a barrier to learners successfully completing their schooling during remote teaching necessitated by the COVID-19 pandemic. My daughter's school district delayed the start of school a week in Fall 2020 as hotspots were backordered. They knew that many learners in the district did not have access to home internet and would not be able to participate in remote teaching without a hotspot and a laptop loaned out by the school. Many college campuses also considered a lack of home internet and worked to extend WiFi into parking lots so students could complete coursework in a car in a school parking lot.

Although these measures likely helped learners continue their education, they are expensive and raise additional questions of equity that cannot be ignored. For example, transportation is a huge issue for many students seeking a college degree, and parking lot WiFi presupposes that learners have access to transportation to get to a parking lot. In my local context in the Central Valley of California, it also raises issues of feasibility. Many days in the beginning of the Fall semester could be well over 100 degrees – not the ideal temperature for studying in a car.

Though there are limitations to providing hotspots and parking lot WiFi, these are important measures that support student learning as many students that rely on smartphones for internet access often use a "workaround ecosystem" in which they use both their smartphones and public WiFi (Pew Research Center, 2016). Just as corporations have turned to omnichannel services that allow consumers to visit online, in-person, and via an app, educational institutions need to ensure learners can access education via multiple channels. This means we can't ignore the smartphones that are often the first thing our students see in the morning and the last thing they see before they go to bed.

Imagine then if students could make use of public resources and mobile-friendly courses to create a flexible learning experience that fits into their lives. As a student, I could wake up and watch my professor's weekly announcement video on my phone in bed before getting my kids ready for school. While they're at school, I could work on an essay on the laptop I borrowed from the university. Then as my kids are playing at the park, I could read for my courses and annotate on my phone. If I had an important test and needed reliable WiFi on a computer, I could use the library as an extra backup to ensure nothing stopped me from achieving my goal of graduating.

The reality is not all our students have access to reliable home internet, but 96% of 18- to 29-year-olds own a smartphone (Pew Research Center, 2021). By designing mobile-friendly courses, we can leverage the technology students already have access to and use frequently to transform access to education. When we design courses that are mobile-friendly, we remove barriers of access for students who do not have reliable internet in their home.

Creating global learning experiences

Mobile-friendly course design also helps to extend learning opportunities across the globe. In 2013, I went backpacking with my husband in Kenya and Uganda. Just four years earlier we had traveled to Thailand and relied on Internet cafes to check-in with our family back home. This time, we had our first smartphones, and it was mind-boggling to use WiFi and be able to stay in touch with our family. We were also amazed to see charging stations everywhere. It didn't matter if it was a small town with only dirt roads –you could find a place to pay a bit to charge your phone.

Although many of these charging stations are not necessarily indicative of smartphone ownership, smartphone ownership is increasingly common across the globe. In a survey of 11 emerging economies, the Pew Research Center found that a majority of adults owned a mobile device and that smartphones were the most commonly owned device (2019b). With increasingly common smartphone ownership for younger generations in emerging economies (Pew Research Center, 2019b), we can increase access to high-quality educational opportunities, if we consider ways in which we can leverage not just smartphones, but also cell phones to support connection and learning.

When considering the potential of mobile design to increase access to education across the world, it is also important to consider how smartphone ownership contrasts with access to the internet. The World Bank estimates that only about 35% of those in emerging economies have access to broadband (2023). Though it stands to reason that while broadband may be technically accessible, it may be prohibitively expensive for many in developing countries as it is for many in the United States. Scholars have noted the potential of mobile learning to support student learning globally (e.g., Farley & Song, 2015). Although integrating mobile-friendly activities is helpful for increasing access to education, mobile design provides a unique opportunity to transform access to education globally through an approach to UDL that acknowledges that students across the world have greater access to mobile devices and use these mobile devices frequently throughout their day.

Serving the so-called nontraditional student

In addition to issues of access, mobile design is an issue of equity as most students in college classes today have multiple demands on their time. The so-called traditional college student who lives on campus, takes courses full-time, and graduates in four years is not the majority student even at four-year resident institutions (Aslanian & Clinefelter, 2012). Instead, a typical student today has responsibilities that include some (if not all) of the following:

- parenting young children and/or taking care of siblings or relatives,
- working a full-time job or multiple jobs, and/or
- commuting to campus.

Designing mobile-friendly courses allows us to better serve students by creating learning experiences with which students can interact fluidly throughout their day. As Cohn (2021) notes "we cannot disparage our students for completing their schoolwork in the ways that work best for maintaining their working lives" (p. 6). Instead, we can leverage the tools our students already have and already use to allow students to interact with coursework in the in-between parts of a day whether they are riding the bus to campus, nursing their baby at 3:00 a.m., or taking a ten-minute break from work.

These in-between parts of a day are called "micromoments" and are already naturally filled with mobile device usage (Adams et al., 2015). These micromoments present an opportunity for students to make consistent progress toward coursework as "90% of smartphone users say they've used their phone to make progress toward a long-term goal ... while out and about" (Adams et al., 2015). Designing mobile-friendly courses allows students to interact with their courses fluidly throughout their day and to use micromoments to make progress in their courses.

In addition, drops in college enrollment indicate a need for educational opportunities in which learners can continue to pursue a degree while they are working full-time jobs. The long-lasting impacts of the pandemic economy indicate a need for courses that fit into learners' lives as they work multiple jobs, balance caregiving demands, or work full-time. With "unprecedented wage growth" for workers in the service industry (Moran, 2021), students may have made the choice to work full-time to support their family during the COVID-19 pandemic. However, in ten years, as their families grow, workers may be looking for flexible learning opportunities to change careers to industries with more potential for growth.

As educators, we are serving learners who are balancing multiple demands on their time. They may be caring for family members or parents. They may be caring for young children. They may be working full-time or working multiple jobs. They may be facing long commutes. For learners balancing work, school, and family, uninterrupted chunks of time may be hard (or impossible) to come by. Students do, however, have in-between parts of their day that can be used for learning when courses are mobile-friendly. When students are able to use their phones to complete a quick reading quiz while waiting to pick up their kids from school, we can remove barriers of access to our courses and support students who are working to transform their lives and the lives of their family through education.

Supporting students experiencing disruptions

Mobile-friendly courses can also help students experiencing disruptions persist in their education. Although students may face many disruptions in the pursuit of their education, two disruptions stand out: campus closures and homelessness. Within the last ten years, we have seen seemingly unimaginable increases in campus closures and in students experiencing homelessness. Though mobile-friendly courses cannot eliminate these disruptions, mobile-friendly courses can offer a helping hand to students as they work to continue their education.

With emergency moves to remote teaching necessitated by the COVID-19 pandemic, it became clear that many learners did not have sufficient access to home internet necessary for completing coursework remotely. Although many campuses have largely returned to offering in-person options, increasing impacts of climate change suggest institutions need to be prepared for temporary moves to remote teaching due to wildfires, mudslides, floods, hurricanes, and other extreme weather events. In these instances, creating courses that are mobile-friendly lower barriers of access that learners face when relying on home internet.

The best way to handle inevitable disruptions to education is to have systems in place in advance of an emergency that help us to communicate to students. In my role in faculty support, I helped faculty transition to fully remote teaching over the course of a weekend in response to the COVID-19 pandemic. In March 2020, I worked with a wide range of faculty who were facing an uncertain future. We didn't know when we would be back on campus. I remember I helped one faculty who had never even used the LMS gradebook. He had all of his grades in a notebook, and he had never used our LMS before. He rose to the challenge, but it took a great deal of work. Although we can hope that we won't face global disruptions to education along the lines of what we experienced during the COVID-19 pandemic, we can help our future selves by being prepared for some level of disruption. Designing mobile-friendly courses can help us to be prepared for disruptions caused by extreme weather events like floods, hurricanes, fires, or mudslides in which students may lose access to the internet in their homes, but in which case students may have smartphones with service.

As educators, we also need to be mindful of disruptions that students may experience in their lives. One disruption students may face is homelessness. About 14% of students experienced homelessness in 2020 in the United States (Soika, 2021). Students who experience homelessness may be couchsurfing or sleeping in campus parking lots (Beckett, 2022). Although experiences of homelessness can vary, education is "a way out of financial instability and stress" (Beckett, 2022) for any student without a place to call home.

Phones offer an important "lifeline to education" (Baldwin & Ching, 2020) to students experiencing homelessness, and many experiencing homelessness may have access to smartphones (Russell, 2019). For young people experiencing homelessness, smartphones are, as the executive director of Larkin Street Youth Services, Sherilyn Adams, noted, "a necessary part of survival" (Russell, 2019). Though data plans are expensive, students experiencing homelessness may rely on public WiFi at libraries or fast-food restaurants to access the internet (Russell, 2019).

Mobile design can be a powerful way for educators to support students experiencing homelessness. A key aspect of mobile design is creating a classroom that signals to students an acceptance of mobile devices for learning. By communicating to students that mobile devices are welcome and encouraged in our courses for learning, we can create an environment that removes any stigma students may feel for relying on their mobile devices for learning. In addition, for students experiencing homelessness, their phone can be an important tool for connection (Rice et al., 2011). By leveraging mobile devices for our courses, we can help students experiencing homeless to not only persist in their degree but also to build connections with us as educators as well as their peers.

Creating mobile-friendly courses cannot fix the disruptions that students face while pursuing their education. A mobile-friendly course will not stop a wildfire or give a student a safe place to sleep. But a mobile-friendly course can help students to persist and continue their education while dealing with disruptions in their lives. For our most vulnerable students, a mobile-friendly course can offer a small helping hand as students work to continue their education.

When we design mobile-friendly courses we can both design for how students already use phones in their personal lives and for students who rely on phones for access to education. Now here is perhaps one of the most important takeaways about mobile design. Mobile design is not an either/or, but rather a journey that we embark on as educators. We do not have to make sure students can complete our course entirely on a phone to transform access to our courses. Making small changes to our courses so that students can complete components of our course on a mobile device can allow a student who is a parent to finish reading an article while they are waiting to pick up their kid from school or a student who is commuting to campus on a bus to watch a short lecture video. By approaching mobile design as a journey and not as a perfect end-outcome, it allows us to play around with how we can design learning experiences for our students so that these learning experiences can fit into their lives and transcend the boundaries of a classroom.

Transforming access through mobile design

Designing mobile-friendly courses transforms access to education by creating a learning environment that encourages 24/7 access through the technology many students already have and use frequently. However, courses are typically not designed for use on mobile devices (Baldwin & Ching, 2020; Wilcox et al., 2016), making it very difficult for students to use their phones to work through course content or submit assignments. In a focus group I conducted on mobile device usage in STEM courses, one student described trying to use a phone for learning as:

> You're crossing the Atlantic and you can be on a big cruise ship, or you can be on a little dingy boat, or you can be in a life vest and the phone's kind of a life vest like yes, you will stay afloat. It's gonna

> suck. It's going to take a long time, hopefully, no sharks get you. That's what I feel like using the phone, if that's your only resource, yes, it can work, it's not ideal, far from ideal.

As educators, embarking on the mobile-design journey can help us to use a UDL approach that makes all learners feel that they are on a cruise ship in our course, no matter what device they are using to complete coursework. Mobile design can help us not just offer learners a lifeline to education but create courses in which phones are one of the many tickets learners can use to embark on the cruise ship and achieve their dreams.

To guide us on the mobile-design journey, this book will explore:

- Why Does Mobile Design Matter?
- How Do I Design Content Learners Can Access on Their Phones?
- How Do I Design Assignments Students Can Complete on Their Phones?
- I've Designed My Mobile-Friendly Course ... Now What?
- What's the Future of Mobile Design?

So, let's get started on our imperfect journey and take that first step toward creating more mobile-friendly courses for our students.

References

Adams, L., Burkholder, E., & Hamilton, K. (2015). Micro-moments: Your guide to winning the shift to mobile. Google. https://www.thinkwithgoogle.com/_qs/documents/34/micromoments-guide-to-winning-shift-to-mobile-download.pdf

Ally, M. (2013). Mobile learning: From research to practice to impact education. *Learning and Teaching in Higher Education: Gulf Perspectives*, *10*(2), 3–12.

Andrews, S., Ellis, D.A., Shaw, H., & Piwek, L. (2015). Beyond self-report: Tools to compare estimated and real-world smartphone use. *PloS One*, *10*(10). 1-9. 10.1371/journal.pone.0139004

Aslanian, C.B., & Clinefelter, D.L. (2012). *Online college students 2012: Comprehensive data on demands and preferences.* The Learning House, Inc.

Attenborough, J.A., & Abbott, S. (2018). Leave them to their own devices: Healthcare students' experiences of using a range of mobile devices for learning. *International Journal for the Scholarship of Teaching and Learning*, *12*(2), 16.

Baldwin, S.J., & Ching, Y.H. (2020). Guidelines for designing online courses for mobile devices. *TechTrends*, *64*(3), 413–422.

Barden, O., & Bygroves, M. (2018). 'I wouldn't be able to graduate if it wasn't for my mobile phone.' The affordances of mobile devices in the construction of complex academic texts. *Innovations in Education and Teaching International*, *55*(5), 555–565. 10.1080/14703297.2017.1322996

Beckett, L. (2022). 'My car is my home': The California students with nowhere to live. *The Guardian*. https://www.theguardian.com/us-news/2022/apr/02/college-students-unhoused-school-help#:~:text=A%202020%20survey%20of%20195%2C000,surfing%E2%80%9D%20or%20staying%20with%20friends

CAST (2018). *The UDL guidelines*. Cast. http://udlguidelines.cast.org

Cohn, J. (2021). *Skim, dive, surface: Teaching digital reading*. West Virginia University Press.

Cochrane, T., & Bateman, R. (2010). Smartphones give you wings: Pedagogical affordances of mobile Web 2.0. *Australasian Journal of Educational Technology*, *26*(1). 10.14742/ajet.1098

Cross, S. (2019). How handheld devices transform, augment and reinforce university students' study habits: Emerging themes from a three-year study. *EDULEARN19 Proceedings*, 6028–6034.

Danish, J., & Hmelo-Silver, C.E. (2020). On activities and affordances for mobile learning. *Contemporary Educational Psychology*, *60*, 101829. 10.1016/j.cedpsych.2019.101829

Eschenbrenner, B., & Nah, F.F.H. (2019). Learning through mobile devices: Leveraging affordances as facilitators of engagement. *International Journal of Mobile Learning and Organisation*, *13*(2), 152–170. 10.1504/ijmlo.2019.098193

Farley, H., & Song, H. (2015). Mobile learning in Southeast Asia: Opportunities and challenges. In Y.A. Zhang (Ed.), *Handbook of mobile teaching and learning*. (pp. 403–419). Springer. 10.1007/978-3-642-54146-9_2

Felisoni, D.D., & Godoi, A.S. (2018). Cell phone usage and academic performance: An experiment. *Computers & Education*, *117*, 175–187. 10.1016/j.compedu.2017.10.006

Harris, H.S., & Greer, M. (2021). Using multimedia for instructor presence in purposeful pedagogy-driven online technical writing courses. *Journal of Technical Writing and Communication*, *51*(1), 31–52. 10.1177/0047281620977162

Kirschner, P.A., & De Bruyckere, P. (2017). The myths of the digital native and the multitasker. *Teaching and Teacher education*, *67*, 135–142. 10.1016/j.tate.2017.06.001

Kobus, M.B., Rietveld, P., & Van Ommeren, J.N. (2013). Ownership versus on-campus use of mobile IT devices by university students. *Computers & Education*, *68*, 29–41. 10.1016/j.compedu.2013.04.003

Moran, A. (2021). An industry's comeback: Service and hospitality jobs see unprecedented wage growth. *Washington Post Jobs*. https://jobs.washingtonpost.com/article/an-industry-s-comeback-service-and-hospitality-jobs-see-unprecedented-wage-growth/

Narayan, V., Herrington, J., & Cochrane, T. (2019). Design principles for heutagogical learning: Implementing student-determined learning with mobile and social media tools. *Australasian Journal of Educational Technology*, *35*(3). 10.14742/ajet.3941

Nasser, R. (2014). Using mobile devices to increase student academic outcomes in Qatar. *Open Journal of Social Sciences*, *2*(02), 67–73. 10.4236/jss.2014.22010

Pew Research Center (2016). Smartphones help those without broadband get online, but don't necessarily bridge the digital divide. https://www.pewresearch.org/fact-tank/2016/10/03/smartphones-help-those-without-broadband-get-online-but-dont-necessarily-bridge-the-digital-divide/

Pew Research Center (2019a). Mobile technology and home broadband 2019. https://www.pewresearch.org/internet/2019/06/13/mobile-technology-and-home-broadband-2019/

Pew Research Center (2019b). Use of smartphones and social media is common across most emerging economies. https://www.pewresearch.org/internet/2019/03/07/use-of-smartphones-and-social-media-is-common-across-most-emerging-economies/

Pew Research Center (2021). Mobile fact sheet. https://www.pewresearch.org/internet/fact-sheet/mobile/

Rice, E., Lee, A., & Taitt, S. (2011). Cell phone use among homeless youth: Potential for new health interventions and research. *Journal of Urban Health*, *88*(6), 1175–1182. 10.1007/s11524-011-9624-z

Russell, M. (2019). Smartphones are a lifeline for the young homeless. If only they had Wi-Fi. San Francisco Chronicle. https://www.sfchronicle.com/business/article/Smartphones-are-a-lifeline-for-the-young-13582809.php

Savin-Badin, M. (2015). *Rethinking learning in an age of digital fluency: Is being digitally tethered a new learning nexus?* Routledge.

Shrider, E.A., Kollar, M., Chen, F., & Semega, J. (2021). *Income and poverty in the United States: 2020*. Census.gov. https://www.census.gov/library/publications/2021/demo/p60-273.html

Soika, B. (2021). The impacts of college student homelessness. USC Rossier. https://rossier.usc.edu/news-insights/news/impacts-college-student-homelessness

Wheelwright, T. (2022). *2022 cell phone usage statistics: How obsessed are we?* Reviews.Org. https://www.reviews.org/mobile/cell-phone-addiction/

Wilcox, D., Thall, J. & Griffin, O. (2016). One Canvas, two audiences: How faculty and students use a newly adopted learning management system. In G. Chamblee & L. Langub (Eds.), *Proceedings of Society for Information Technology & Teacher Education International Conference* (pp. 1163–1168). Savannah, GA, United States: Association for the Advancement of Computing in Education (AACE). https://www.learntechlib.org/primary/p/171838/

World Bank. (2023). Connecting for inclusion: Broadband access for all. https://www.worldbank.org/en/topic/digitaldevelopment/brief/connecting-for-inclusion-broadband-access-for-all#:~:text=Only%20about%2035%20percent%20of,facilitated%20by%20new%20wireless%20technologies

2

THE MOBILE-FRIENDLY COURSE CONTINUUM

DEMYSTIFYING MOBILE DESIGN

The mobile-friendly course continuum

Many of the recommendations educators receive are either/ors. In the realm of professional development, educators are rarely presented with opportunities to adapt recommendations along a continuum that best suits their teaching style, learners, and unique institutional context. Let's consider accessibility for a moment. As educators, we are often taught that an image either has alternative text or it doesn't. In actuality, crafting alternative text is an art form in which we can constantly develop our skills to best serve our learners and institutional context. For example, if I am in California and crafting alternative text for an image of a wildfire, I would be mindful of learners who may have personally experienced trauma or loss from a wildfire. In this case, alt text is not an either/or, but rather an opportunity to refine my practice as an educator to best serve my local students.

The art of teaching lies in the journey – the journey in which we as educators constantly reflect and refine our practice to best serve and reach

DOI: 10.4324/9781003328773-3

our students. Creating a mobile-friendly course is a journey that begins with a reflection on the needs of our learners and how learners use mobile devices in their daily lives. Depending on the makeup of our particular classes and campuses, mobile-friendly courses may benefit learners who are:

- experiencing homelessness,
- taking care of children or relatives,
- working multiple jobs,
- balancing demanding academic schedules,
- traveling for sports,
- dealing with disruptions to education caused by displacement due to conflicts or climate change, and/or
- relying on phones for home internet.

For each of these students, mobile-friendly courses can help them persist in their education.

As Baldwin and Ching (2020) noted, "for some students, mobile devices are a lifeline to education" (p. 420). In Chapter 1, we explored in detail how mobile-friendly course design is an issue of equity. Creating mobile-friendly courses allows us as educators to design for equity and serve students who rely on the technology they carry in their pockets.

After reflecting on the "why" of mobile design, we can continue on the journey of designing mobile-friendly courses by implementing small changes that allow us to move our courses across a continuum of mobile-friendliness. Mobile design is not an either/or, but rather a series of small steps that make our courses easier and more enjoyable to interact with on a mobile device. (Table 2.1)

The mobile design continuum unpacks the components of a mobile-friendly course into two categories: course content and assignments. For each of these, we can take small steps to move our courses from not very mobile-friendly to very mobile-friendly as appropriate. The continuum also takes into account local requirements that may be outside of our control as educators. For example, I was working with a history professor on designing a mobile-friendly course. The particular course she was designing had a 10,000-word essay requirement. Although some students may write long essays on their phones, typing an essay on a phone

Table 2.1 Mobile-friendly course continuum.

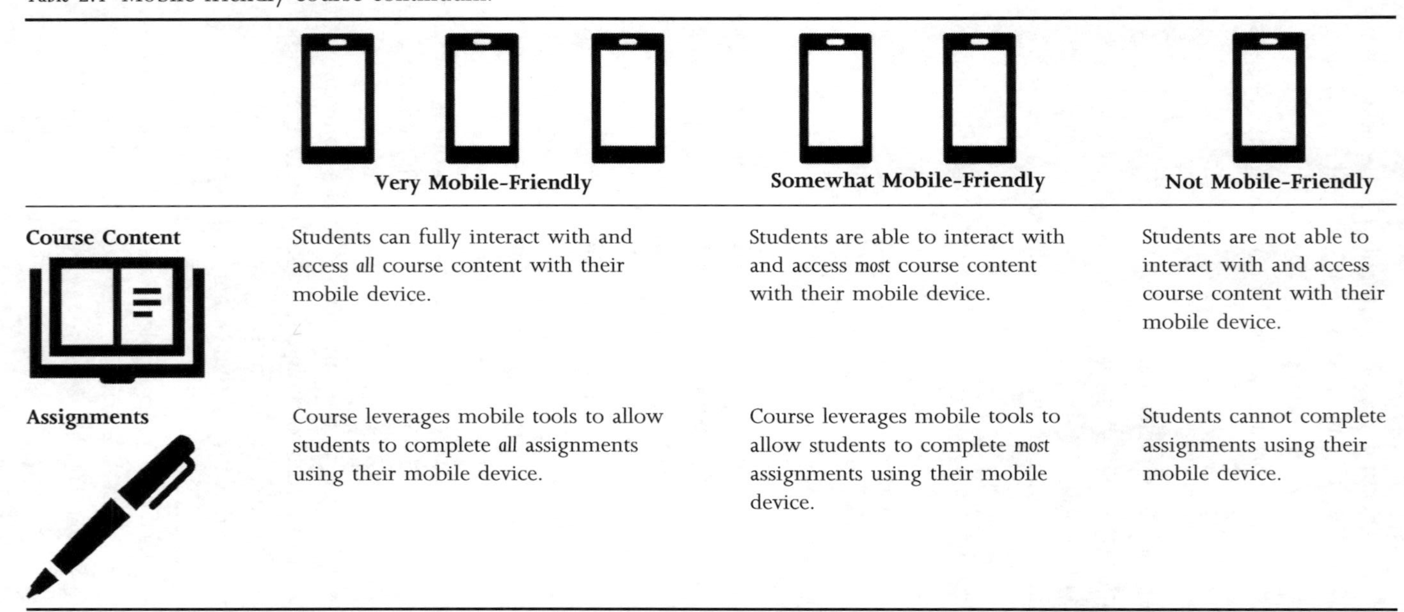

	Very Mobile-Friendly	Somewhat Mobile-Friendly	Not Mobile-Friendly
Course Content	Students can fully interact with and access *all* course content with their mobile device.	Students are able to interact with and access *most* course content with their mobile device.	Students are not able to interact with and access course content with their mobile device.
Assignments	Course leverages mobile tools to allow students to complete *all* assignments using their mobile device.	Course leverages mobile tools to allow students to complete *most* assignments using their mobile device.	Students cannot complete assignments using their mobile device.

is certainly not easy. In this case, due to curriculum requirements outside of her control, she was not able to make all the assignments in her course mobile-friendly. However, she was able to make her course content mobile-friendly so that students could read articles and interact with course lectures on their phones. By envisioning mobile design as a continuum that separates course content and assignments, she was able to still implement small steps to make her course content mobile-friendly. However, if mobile design was presented as an either/or, she would likely have abandoned the pursuit of creating a mobile-friendly course due to the essay requirement.

Demystifying mobile design

Creating a course that students can complete successfully on their mobile devices may feel like a complicated and mystical task. It can be difficult to imagine where to begin as often we as educators design courses on computers, not on mobile devices. Fortunately, designing mobile-friendly courses does not have to be complicated. Instead, we can design mobile-friendly courses by taking a series of small steps that work to maximize the benefits of mobile devices for learning while mitigating the limitations.

To demystify mobile design, we must first understand the benefits and limitations of mobile devices for learning. Technologies are not neutral (Neal, 2011), and as such an informed understanding of the affordances and constraints of technologies can help to support mindful implementation and the design of courses that leverage the unique benefits of mobile devices for learning.

Benefits of mobile devices

Reflecting on how we use phones in our everyday lives can help to illuminate some of the benefits of mobile devices (Box 2.1).

BOX 2.1 REFLECTION

Take a moment to reflect on how you use your mobile device in your daily life. In what ways does your phone make your life easier?

During the work week, my smartphone certainly makes my life easier. Three days a week the alarm goes off early so I can go for a run and listen to podcasts on my phone. Then the alarm goes off again to give my daughter a ten-minute warning that we need to be almost ready to go to school. And ten minutes later the alarm goes off again to let us know it is actually time to go to school. After dropping off my daughter, I use my phone to call my mom on my way to work. Then at work, I can stay connected to colleagues when I go for a walk around campus so I can respond to emergency notifications. I also know that if my daughter gets sick, I will get a call from her school, and I can make sure either my husband or my mom picks her up. When I reflect on my phone use during a workday, my phone offers clear benefits for managing my time and supporting connection with my family and colleagues.

As we discussed in Chapter 1, when we look at the research on mobile devices, scholars have noted these benefits and more, including:

- anytime/anywhere learning (Ally, 2013; Barden & Bygroves, 2018),
- portability (Attenborough & Abbott, 2018; Kobus et al., 2013),
- convenience (Barden & Bygroves, 2018),
- multimodal capabilities (Cochrane & Bateman, 2010), and
- connection (Cochrane & Bateman, 2010; Cross, 2019; Danish & Hmelo-Silver, 2020; Nasser, 2014).

Let's dig into these affordances. One benefit of mobile devices is the anytime/anywhere learning that they afford students (Ally, 2013). Mobile devices support anytime/anywhere learning that transcends the boundaries of a physical space and even time (Barden & Bygroves, 2018). Anytime/anywhere learning can support student learning by encouraging consistent engagement with a concept beyond the confines of a classroom and concentrated chunks of time spent on a computer. Enabling anytime/anywhere learning has exciting implications for supporting students in tackling complicated and difficult tasks. From personal finance to exercise to learning, we know that we will be able to achieve greater results if we can make small amounts of progress each day. I will be in better shape if I exercise a bit each day as opposed to a long and intense workout session every few weeks. As educators, we have seen first-hand that students are more successful in our courses when they spend time studying and reviewing each day. We encourage students to set aside time to focus on our course each day (or week) instead of cramming at the end of the semester. Mobile devices provide an exciting opportunity to support consistent attention to our coursework through anytime/anywhere learning as students already likely carry their mobile device with them everywhere they go.

Perhaps one of the most commonly recognized benefits of mobile devices is portability. Although laptops are arguably portable, students may find it "cumbersome" to carry a laptop with them (Kobus et al., 2013, p. 36). The small size and lightweight nature of mobile devices make it easier for students to carry them (Attenborough & Abbott, 2018). Additionally, the portability of mobile devices offers obvious benefits for students who may be experiencing displacement as refugees or who have had to evacuate due to extreme weather events such as fires or floods.

Mobile devices also offer a certain level of convenience. Even if students have access to computers, they may prefer to use their phones for quick tasks. Barden and Bygroves (2018) noted laptops were perceived as being "slow and cumbersome" (Barden & Bygroves, 2018, p. 560). In a focus group on mobile device use I conducted with students, they also noted computers could be inconvenient. As one student described it:

> If I didn't have my phone, I probably wouldn't be checking my email nearly as much or staying focused on my stuff. Because yeah I just sometimes pull it out, look. I'm like okay, any emails, any updates from my class, but if I had to deal with my computer all the time. I don't like pulling my computer out as it's kind of old and it takes a while to load up.

For some of our students, using a mobile device offers a preferable alternative for quick tasks. Instead of having to wait for an older computer to turn on, students can use their phones to quickly check emails and updates from their instructor.

Mobile devices also often include sophisticated multimodal capabilities that make it easy for students to record videos and take high-quality photos. Mobile devices offer a unique opportunity for students to create their own images and/or videos to create highly localized and meaningful assignments. Highlighting student voices and creating spaces for students to center their experiences and values in our courses is a fundamental component of equity-minded pedagogy. In an equity-minded course, "students must see themselves in their learning" (Muhammad, 2020, p. 69). Barden and Bygroves' (2018) found in their exploratory case study that a student was able to make use of local inspiration to complete sophisticated and personally meaningful assignments with the use of a mobile device. By leveraging the multimodal capabilities of mobile devices, we as educators can design assignments in which students can center their lived experiences and identities.

Finally, mobile devices offer an important opportunity for students to connect with instructors and other students. As educators, the relationships we build with our students are deeply profound, and I'm sure many of us can recall moments where we witnessed first-hand the power of relationships for learning. We have seen how incredibly hard students will work when they know we care for them and are invested in their success. Research supports our experience as educators and shows that strong instructor–student relationships support student learning (Cung et al., 2018, Sher, 2009), satisfaction (Sher, 2009), and retention (Mitchell & Hughes, 2014). Scholars note time and again that relationships are the foundation for teaching (Dobransky & Frymier, 2004; Hoffman, 2014; Strachan, 2020). As educators, the heart of our practice is the relationships we build with students.

Leveraging mobile devices for learning can build relationships in two ways. First, as students almost always have their mobile devices with them, these devices provide an important and meaningful way for educators to consistently check in with students. Intuitively, we know as educators that seeing students at the grocery store or out in the community helps to build trust and relationships with students. Scholars have supported this intuition with research suggesting that out-of-class communication between students and educators not only builds trust (Dobransky & Frymier, 2004; Jaasma & Koper, 1999), but also supports increased learning (Dobransky & Frymier, 2004). Mobile devices provide a unique opportunity for educators to communicate easily with students out of the classroom. Leveraging texting to send frequent reminders can help educators and students bond (Rau et al., 2008), and increase student learning (Nasser, 2014). Second, creating a course in which students can use their mobile devices to complete assignments and access course content can create a welcoming and inclusive environment that helps to alleviate some of the shame students may feel as they rely on mobile devices for schoolwork. Communicating to students that mobile devices are welcome and that particular components of a course are especially mobile-friendly can signal to students that they are welcome in the course and that the way they use technology is welcome.

Anytime/anywhere learning, portability, convenience, multimodal capabilities, and connection represent some of the many benefits of mobile devices for supporting student learning. Research also suggests additional benefits of mobile devices may include flexibility and efficiency (Cross, 2019). All in all, these benefits provide a helpful foundation upon which we can consider how to leverage and maximize these affordances in mobile design. However, we also need to be aware of the limitations of mobile devices to effectively design mobile-friendly courses.

Limitations of mobile devices

Reflecting on our day-to-day phone use can also help us to explore some of the limitations of mobile devices (Box 2.2).

BOX 2.2 REFLECTION

Now take a moment to reflect on the limitations of your phone. In what ways does your phone make your life more difficult or what tasks are more difficult on your phone?

For me, one of the biggest limitations of my phone has been its pull for my attention. When I am spending time with my daughter, the ding of my phone will take me out of the moment with her and make me focus on a notification from Instagram. If I'm trying to write and my phone buzzes, it can be difficult for me to regain my focus. My experience is not uncommon, and research suggests that some common constraints of mobile devices include:

- attention pulling (Barden & Bygroves, 2018),
- small screens (Eschenbrenner & Nah, 2019), and

- negative perceptions of mobile device usage for learning (Ally, 2013; Barden & Bygroves, 2018).

Let's start with the distractibility factor. Although it may be more difficult to multitask on a mobile device, frequent notifications from social media or texts can pull attention away from coursework and make it difficult for students to focus on coursework if they are using a smartphone. In Chapter 1, we explored the concept of "digital tethering" that characterizes the strong pull of mobile devices in our lives (Savin-Badin, 2015, p. 1). Savin-Badin (2015) does not claim that digital tethering is strictly a limitation of mobile devices, but rather a complex phenomenon with both positives and negatives for student learning and engagement. Barden & Bygroves (2018) noted in their exploratory case study that being tethered to a device held both benefits and limitations. For instance, while tethering presented important opportunities for anytime/anywhere that supported the creation of a sophisticated text, it also presented limitations such as "feeling frazzled" and socially isolated (Barden & Bygroves, 2018, p. 563). As educators, though, we have a unique opportunity to guide students in managing the pull of their mobile devices in ways that will support their education, careers, and personal lives. The pull of mobile devices is not unique to educational contexts, and as such, managing the pull of mobile devices is an important 21st-century skill that students need to master to lead productive and fulfilling lives.

We can teach students easy ways to manage the pull of mobile devices by encouraging students to turn off notifications when they are engaging in schoolwork or want to focus on important relationships. By recognizing the pull of mobile devices as a complicated limitation, we can offer students much-needed direct instruction and guidance on how to manage the pull on their attention in ways that will benefit their lives. However, if we categorize mobile devices as inappropriate for learning due to this limitation, we are doing a disservice to our students as they will need to manage this pull to be successful and happy in their lives. Many educators have likely developed strategies for managing the pull of mobile devices in their own lives. After my four-year-old started getting frustrated because I was looking at my phone while we were watching a movie, I set the do-not-disturb feature on my phone to turn on every evening at 6 p.m. I also started leaving my phone in a different room. Our phones and the apps on them are often designed to get our attention, and if we don't actively apply strategies to counteract this pulling of our attention, phones will easily do what they are designed to do: grab our attention every few seconds. Sharing the strategies we have developed ourselves can help students manage the pull of their mobile devices in ways that will benefit not only their learning, but also their work and personal lives.

Another limitation of mobile devices is the small screen. Small screens are often listed as a major constraint of mobile devices that limit their effectiveness for learning (Baldwin & Ching, 2020; Eschenbrenner & Nah, 2019). However, this particular limitation may also offer some unique benefits to using mobile devices for learning as it is often more difficult to multitask on a mobile device. In addition, design strategies such as chunking content, keeping pages short, and using a 14-point font can help to minimize the limitation of small screens and manage demands on cognitive load (Eschenbrenner & Nah, 2019).

Finally, perhaps one of the largest constraints of mobile devices is a shared perception by educators and students that students shouldn't be using phones for learning. By the time students enter college, they have likely experienced years of bans on cell phones in the classroom. Although smartphone ownership has increased significantly since 2011 (Pew Research Center, 2021), mobile devices continue to be banned in K–16 courses (Jones et al., 2020). Historically, there has been a huge focus on how to keep phones out of our classrooms and potentially negatively impacting student learning. But technologies are nuanced. Just as Plato's Socrates feared the emerging technology of writing and its impact on society and the brain (Ong, 2002), a common trope about mobile devices is that they take away from student learning if used in the classroom.

Many students have internalized this negative framing of cell phone use for learning. In one study, a student was embarrassed about using a phone to complete schoolwork and so pretended to be texting instead of working on his assignment. As he said, "I sometimes was worried in lectures because I felt a bit embarrassed working off my phone in lectures so I often do it under the table it looks like I'm texting" (Barden & Bygroves, 2018, p. 561). In this case, the student would rather appear to be using the phone for an accepted purpose (texting) than to deviate from this and use the phone for learning.

The myth of the digital native is that students today are more adept at using technologies. However, though students may know how to stream Netflix or post on TikTok, they need guidance and support on how to use mobile devices for learning. Although my daughter learned at an early age how to watch Daniel Tiger on her iPad, she needed her kindergarten teacher to guide her on how to use Jamboard for learning.

Although Plato's Socrates feared the technology of writing, it transformed access to knowledge and education. Just like writing, mobile devices have the potential to democratize learning in seemingly unprecedented ways. Thanks to the written word, I can gain insight from great thinkers across the world and across time. With the near ubiquity of mobile devices, we have the potential to leverage this tool to deliver content to our students, but also, more importantly, to allow our students to contribute their own voices to not only our classes, but also to global conversations.

Many of our students are trying to (or would want to) complete coursework on their phones, but our courses are not made for phones. We know as educators that we support student success when we are responsive to our students, who they are, and what they need. By designing mobile-friendly courses, we are creating learning experiences that are responsive to the technology students have and how they already use it. As with all technologies, acknowledging the benefits and limitations allows us to design our courses in ways that maximize the affordances while mitigating the constraints. Currently, educators typically design courses with the idea that students are completing coursework on their laptops when in actuality students are using mobile devices or using some combination of laptops and mobile devices (Baldwin & Ching, 2020). Designing courses without attending to mobile design maximizes the limitations of mobile devices without realizing the benefits of phones for learning.

Small steps to maximize the benefits of mobile devices

The mobile-friendly course continuum allows us to apply different strategies for creating mobile-friendly course content and mobile-friendly assignments. By mindfully designing with consideration for the benefits and limitations of mobile devices, we can create a course that facilitates learning whether a student is using a smartphone or a computer.

Designing mobile-friendly course content

The strategies for designing mobile-friendly course content fall under three guiding principles that work to mitigate the limitations of mobile devices while maximizing the benefits. These principles are:

1. Create Content for Small Screens
2. Built Trust
3. Leverage Moments

By taking small steps to make pages shorter, embed videos, and add headings, students can more easily complete readings, watch videos, and interact with course content without being limited by a 5-inch screen. Creating content for small screens allows us to not only serve students who rely on their phones to complete schoolwork or need to make use of their ten-minute break, but also to serve all students by chunking content to manage cognitive load (Eschenbrenner & Nah, 2019).

Meaningful instructor–student relationships have a profound impact on student learning. But we can't have a relationship without trust. While trust can support student learning in big ways, it is often built through small actions. Mobile-friendly course design presents an opportunity to build trust with students through small actions that show care, understanding, and acceptance.

Leveraging moments allows us to design content that can be completed in the in-between moments of a day. This allows us to create courses that align with how students are already using mobile devices for learning. Students tend to use mobile devices frequently throughout the day (Andrews et al., 2015), but for shorter intervals than a computer or laptop (López & Silva, 2014). By chunking content into sections that can be completed in ten minutes or less, we can design courses that align with how students are already using mobile devices to support students who are juggling heavy academic loads, long commutes, and childcare.

Designing mobile-friendly assignments

The strategies for designing mobile-friendly assignments fall under the following three guiding principles:

1. Allow Choice
2. Integrate Multimodality
3. Leverage Mobile-Friendly Tools

Allowing student choice is perhaps the easiest way to create mobile-friendly assignments as it can often entail simply offering an additional way students can submit an assignment. For example, in Calculus instead of requiring that students download a Word document with practice problems, type their answers on a computer, and then upload it, educators can offer the option for students to write their answers on a sheet of paper, scan it with their phone, and then upload their responses. This small step requires very little additional effort on behalf of the instructor but can have an outsized impact on students who don't have access to home internet. In this instance, it also helps to mitigate the limitation of the small screen as students could turn their phones sideways and zoom in to see one question at a time while working through the practice problems on a larger sheet of paper.

Integrating multimodal assignments provides an opportunity to leverage an important benefit of mobile devices: the built-in capabilities for creating images, audio, and/or video. An added benefit of leveraging multimodal assignments is it can also highlight the anytime/anywhere and portability benefits of mobile devices. Perhaps one of the most exciting aspects of this principle is the potential that multimodal assignments have for leveraging so many benefits of mobile devices to extend learning beyond the classroom and even chunks of time in front of a computer. Multimodal assignments can encourage students to look around themselves in their daily lives for inspiration and connection to what they are learning.

Leveraging mobile-friendly tools helps educators work smarter, not harder. When educators choose tools that are already mobile-friendly, it accelerates the process of mobile-friendly design. Choosing tools that are mobile-friendly is like taking the moving walkway at the airport; it just eliminates a lot of steps in designing mobile-friendly assignments. It also helps to continue to remove the negative perceptions of using mobile devices for learning. Mobile-friendly tools work well on laptops and mobile devices, and they often include affirmative visuals of the tool on mobile devices, inclusive directions, and help documentation that work for computers or mobile devices.

As educators, we can take small steps to enact these principles of mobile-friendly design to create courses in which students can use their mobile device or computer. The following chapters will explore each of these principles and will include evidence-based actionable recommendations we can apply to our practice as educators.

The transformative power of the mobile design journey

The mobile design continuum allows us to take small steps to make the content and assignments of our courses more mobile-friendly. Approaching mobile design as a continuum rather than an either/or supports the iterative nature of teaching and allows educators to make small changes to their courses. The small steps educators make towards creating mobile-friendly courses can have a transformative impact on not only how students access our courses, but also how our courses fit into students' lives. The transformative power of the mobile design journey lies in the journey itself. The first step of this journey begins with a move from creating courses based on how we think students should use technology to creating courses based on how students actually use technology. Leveraging the tools students already use and offering some guidance on how to use these tools to succeed in school provides a solid foundation upon which we can build mobile-friendly courses to better support student learning. By designing mobile-friendly courses, we can create a welcoming environment upon which we can leverage mobile devices to build relationships with students and send signals of belonging. Mobile-friendly design allows us to create an inclusive environment for all students regardless of which device they use, where they live, or what they are balancing in their personal, professional, and academic lives.

References

Ally, M. (2013). Mobile learning: From research to practice to impact education. *Learning and Teaching in Higher Education: Gulf Perspectives*, *10*(2), 3–12.

Andrews, S., Ellis, D.A., Shaw, H., & Piwek, L. (2015). Beyond self-report: Tools to compare estimated and real-world smartphone use. *PloS One*, *10*(10). 1–9. 10.1371/journal.pone.0139004

Attenborough, J.A., & Abbott, S. (2018). Leave them to their own devices: Healthcare students' experiences of using a range of mobile devices for learning. *International Journal for the Scholarship of Teaching and Learning*, *12*(2), 16.

Baldwin, S.J., & Ching, Y.H. (2020). Guidelines for designing online courses for mobile devices. *TechTrends*, *64*(3), 413–422.

Barden, O., & Bygroves, M. (2018). 'I wouldn't be able to graduate if it wasn't for my mobile phone.' The affordances of mobile devices in the construction of complex academic texts. *Innovations in Education and Teaching International*, *55*(5), 555–565. 10.1080/14703297.2017.1322996

Cochrane, T., & Bateman, R. (2010). Smartphones give you wings: Pedagogical affordances of mobile Web 2.0. *Australasian Journal of Educational Technology*, *26*(1). 10.14742/ajet.1098

Cross, S. (2019). How handheld devices transform, augment and reinforce university students' study habits: emerging themes from a three-year study. *EDULEARN19 Proceedings*, 6028–6034.

Cung, B., Xu, D., & Eichhorn, S. (2018). Increasing interpersonal interactions in an online course: Does increased instructor email activity and voluntary meeting time in a physical classroom facilitate student learning?. *Online Learning*, *22*(3), 193–215.

Danish, J., & Hmelo-Silver, C.E. (2020). On activities and affordances for mobile learning. *Contemporary Educational Psychology*, *60*, 101829. 10.1016/j.cedpsych.2019.101829

Dobransky, N.D., & Frymier, A.B. (2004). Developing teacher-student relationships through out of class communication. *Communication Quarterly*, *52*(3), 211–223. 10.1080/01463370409370193

Eschenbrenner, B., & Nah, F.F.H. (2019). Learning through mobile devices: Leveraging affordances as facilitators of engagement. *International Journal of Mobile Learning and Organisation*, *13*(2), 152–170. 10.1504/ijmlo.2019.098193

Hoffman, E.M. (2014). Faculty and student relationships: Context matters. *College Teaching, 62*(1), 13–19. https://www.jstor.org/stable/24760532

Jaasma, M.A., & Koper, R.J. (1999) The relationship of student-faculty out-of-class communication to instructor immediacy and trust and to student motivation, *Communication Education, 48*(1), 41–47. 10.1080/03634529909379151

Jones, S.B., Aruguete, M.S., & Gretlein, R. (2020). Cell phone use policies in the college classroom: Do they work?. *Transactions of the Missouri Academy of Science, 48*(2020), 5–9. 10.30956/MAS-31R1

Kobus, M.B., Rietveld, P., & Van Ommeren, J.N. (2013). Ownership versus on-campus use of mobile IT devices by university students. *Computers & Education, 68*, 29–41. 10.1016/j.compedu.2013.04.003

López, F.A. & Silva, M.M. (2014). M-learning patterns in the virtual classroom. *Mobile Learning Applications in Higher Education, 11*(1), 208–221.

Mitchell, Y.F., & Hughes, G.D. (2014). Demographic and instructor-student interaction factors associated with community college students' intent to persist. *Journal of Research in Education, 24*(2), 63–78.

Muhammad, G. (2020). *Cultivating genius: An equity framework for culturally and historically responsive literacy*. Scholastic.

Nasser, R. (2014). Using mobile devices to increase student academic outcomes in Qatar. *Open Journal of Social Sciences, 2*(02), 67–73. 10.4236/jss.2014.22010

Neal, M.R. (2011). *Writing assessment and the revolution in digital texts and technologies*. Teachers College Press.

Ong, W. (2002). *Orality and literacy*. (2nd ed.). Routledge.

Pew Research Center (2021). Mobile fact sheet. https://www.pewresearch.org/internet/fact-sheet/mobile/

Rau, P.L.P., Gao, Q., & Wu, L.M. (2008). Using mobile communication technology in high school education: Motivation, pressure, and learning performance. *Computers & Education, 50*(1), 1–22. 10.1016/j.compedu.2006.03.008

Savin-Badin, M. (2015). *Rethinking learning in an age of digital fluency: Is being digitally tethered a new learning nexus?* Routledge.

Sher, A. (2009). Assessing the relationship of student-instructor and student-student interaction to student learning and satisfaction in web-based online learning environment. *Journal of Interactive Online Learning, 8*(2),102–120.

Strachan, S.L. (2020). The case for the caring instructor. *College Teaching, 68*(2), 53–56. 10.1080/87567555.2019.1711011

PART 2

HOW DO I DESIGN CONTENT STUDENTS CAN ACCESS ON THEIR PHONES?

3

CREATE CONTENT FOR SMALL SCREENS

MOBILE DESIGN MEETS ACCESSIBILITY

The challenge of small screens

One of the biggest challenges in designing mobile-friendly courses is overcoming the limitation of small screens. In our day-to-day lives, it is likely we have encountered this limitation. When I have tried to use websites not designed for mobile use, I typically abandon my phone and open the website instead on a computer. For students, the small screen can be particularly problematic when course pages are not designed to be viewed on a mobile device. When faced with the endless scroll of long pages a student may be deterred from viewing course content on a phone. However, not all students have a computer or laptop they can turn to when frustrated with accessing course content on their phone. Students may abandon accessing course content altogether if they:

- rely on an older computer that takes a long time to turn on or load,

DOI: 10.4324/9781003328773-5

- share a computer with family, and/or
- try to fit their studies into a schedule packed with childcare and work.

For these students, creating content that is accessible on small screens can mean the difference between completing that week's readings or not. Fortunately, we can design course content for small screens by making use of strategies that also help us to meet accessibility guidelines.

The first mobile design principle provides actionable strategies we as educators can implement to design content for small screens. Many of these strategies are already recommendations we may have received to ensure our course content is accessible to students with disabilities. By leveraging these strategies, we can mitigate the limitation of small screens.

Mobile design principle #1: Create content for small screens

The first mobile design principle focuses on how we can create content for small screens. The best place to start in designing mobile-friendly course content is to consider the double-duty strategies that serve both students with disabilities and students accessing courses on mobile devices. Many of these strategies are recommendations for creating accessible course content of which we may have already heard, or we may already be implementing. These strategies are simple steps we can begin (or continue) to implement in our courses to create a course that not only mitigates the limitation of a small screen, but also transforms the small screen of a mobile device into a powerful tool that students can use to help encourage focus and concentration.

Chunking content to manage cognitive load

In our everyday lives, we are surrounded by institutionalized practices that break information up into smaller, more manageable chunks to help us remember. We don't remember phone numbers by memorizing ten digits, but rather we memorize phone numbers in chunks of three and four numbers. Chunking content into small, manageable components can help to reduce the demands on cognitive load (Major & Calandrino, 2018) and can help students with disabilities and hard-to-diagnose disabilities process course content (Web Accessibility Initiative, 2022a). Chunking content not only helps to reduce cognitive load, but also transforms the limitation of a smaller screen into a benefit as it can help students to focus on a singular task (Eschenbrenner & Nah, 2019).

The first step to chunk content in our course is to focus on the larger units that make up a course. LMSs typically include a feature in which instructors can organize their courses into modules. As instructors, we can choose to create modules based on themes (e.g., The Limbic System) or weeks (e.g., Week 1). Using modules is an effective strategy for creating mobile-friendly course content (Seilhamer et al., 2020). Modules can help to mitigate the limitation of a small screen as modules allow students to get a sense of the course as a whole while also allowing students to zoom into one module to see what they need to complete that week. Chunking content into modules has also been shown to increase completion rates, learning, and retention of learning when compared to a course without modules (Méndez-Carbajo & Wolla, 2019). Modules also provide an important opportunity for instructors to create a sense of consistency that can reduce stress for students as they don't have to relearn how to navigate the course each week. To take it a step further, some LMSs allow instructors to add headers to a module so the pages within a particular module are chunked. This is especially helpful for modules with a lot of content.

After we have chunked our course into modules, we can consider ways in which we can chunk content on pages within that module. Adding headers to a page can help to chunk content on a page and signal to students what we want them to take away from the course. This strategy can be an effective approach to creating mobile-friendly courses (Seilhamer et al., 2020). Headers are also an important component of creating accessible course content as headers help to make a course easier to navigate for students using screen readers. Headers can also be used to create a sense of consistency. For example, if I add an overview page to each module, I can use the same headers on each overview page throughout the course, so students know what to expect. I can also use headers to signal to students what I want them to take away from that page. In Figure 3.1, the headers make it clear that the overall message on this page is how to have a healthy diet.

Just looking at the headers gives a sense of the content of the course as well as the takeaway I want for my students: to understand how to have a healthy diet. Compare this to a page with the headers in Figure 3.2.

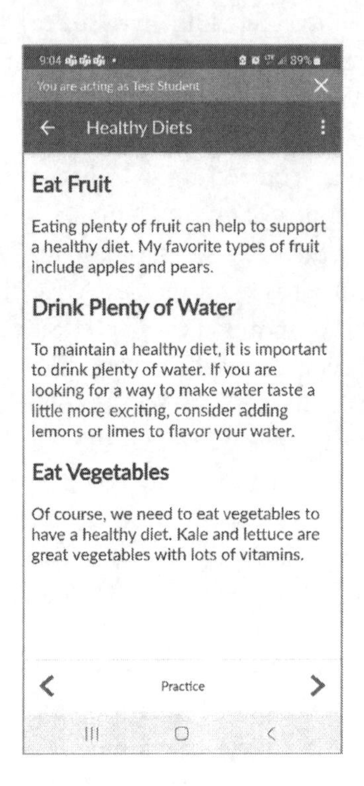

Figure 3.1 Using headers to chunk content and communicate meaning: Healthy diets.

In each of these examples, I only refer to apples, pears, lemons, limes, lettuce, and kale. However, one page offers advice on how to have a healthy diet, whereas the other includes recipes with tempting desserts. The headers in both figures help to signal to the student what the big takeaway is from that page. This optimizes the content for mobile devices as it allows students to easily get a sense of the overall message of a page at a glance.

Sometimes, though, we may have so much content on a page that students may feel overwhelmed by a seemingly endless scroll and a page filled with paragraph after paragraph. This is especially true in online courses or courses in which we are using Open Educational Resources and we have a lot of content integrated directly into the pages of our LMSs. In this case, headers won't be enough to prevent students from being overwhelmed by long pages. As a solution, we can use accordions

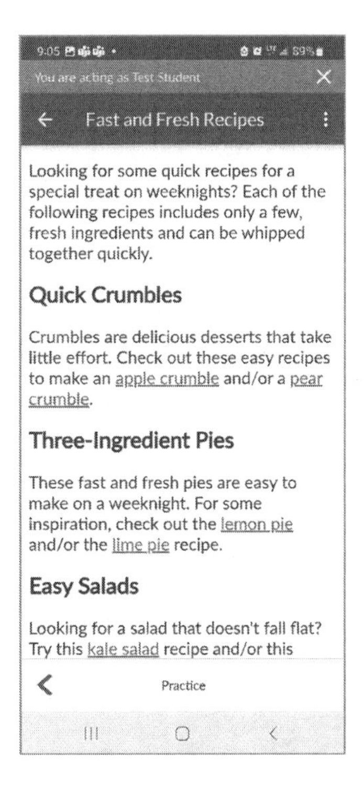

Figure 3.2 Using headers to chunk content and communicate meaning: Fast and fresh recipes.

or tabs to further chunk the content. This allows students to toggle back and forth between content sections so they can more easily access the course on a small screen, as seen in Figure 3.3. In this instance, instead of including links for the recipes, I can use accordions to embed the recipes directly on the page. Students can still easily condense the accordions so they are able to see all three accordions at once or they can expand the accordions to see a particular recipe.

Depending on your institution's LMS and software licensing, you may have access to tools that can make adding accordions or tabs to a page relatively easy. However, it is also possible to do a Google search to find HTML code to create your own accordions or tabs. Just be mindful to follow guidelines to create accordions and/or tabs that are navigable by a keyboard to ensure content is accessible to students with disabilities (Web Accessibility Initiative, 2022b).

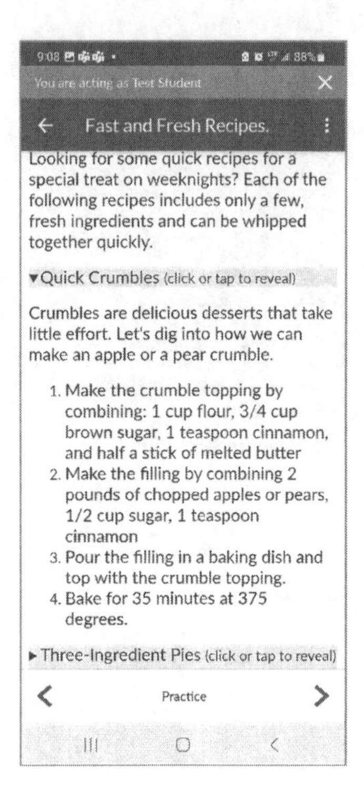

Figure 3.3 Using accordions to chunk long content.

Creating a visually appealing and accessible experience

After we have focused on chunking content, we can turn our attention to creating a visually appealing experience while simultaneously creating accessible course materials. Visually appealing design is especially important on mobile devices as the design choices we make can either reduce the inconvenience of a small screen or amplify it. Creating a visually appealing course is also important for student learning. Research suggests that aesthetic course design can decrease cognitive load and increase student satisfaction and performance (Miller, 2011). Without formal training in design though, it can be intimidating to imagine how we can create a visually appealing course for our students. Luckily, there are some basic strategies we can implement that will not only help to make our courses more visually appealing across devices, but will also help to make them accessible to students with disabilities.

Let's start off with tables. If a table is used to design the layout of a page, the page can appear wonky when viewed on a mobile device. Removing unnecessary tables can be a helpful strategy for students using mobile devices as the table doesn't translate well to a small screen (Baldwin & Ching, 2020). Reserving the use of tables for data is also a helpful double-duty strategy as the information in tables can be confusing when read by a screen reader (WebAIM, 2018). For example, let's say I use a table to communicate to students my office hours for the week. Using the "Read Aloud" feature in Microsoft Word a student would hear:

> Monday Tuesday Wednesday Thursday Friday Time 1 3 p m 9 11 a m No office hours 7 9 p m 12 1 p m Location Zoom room My office C35 Zoom room My office C35.

Without following specific steps to indicate reading order in a table, the information will be read by rows instead of columns (Box 3.1).

BOX 3.1 REFLECTION

Let's take a moment to reflect. Based on this information, what is the time and location for my office hours on Thursdays?

Now let's look at my office hours in Table 3.1. Were you able to accurately determine the location and time of my office hours? I'm guessing if you were able to figure out the time and location of my office hours, it took some time and effort as the table was read line by line.

After running the accessibility checker in Microsoft Word, I received a "Warning" indicating a need to split the office hours cells instead of having those merged. Once the cells were split, the document passed the

Table 3.1 Weekly office hours.

	Monday	*Tuesday*	*Wednesday*	*Thursday*	*Friday*
Time	1–3 p.m.	9–11 a.m.	No office hours	7–9 p.m.	12-1 p.m.
Location	Zoom room	My office: C35		Zoom room	My office: C35

Accessibility Check; however, the table still read the information row by row. Although tables can be made accessible for students using a screen reader with the use of header rows, it can be difficult and time-consuming to ensure that all tables are accurately read by a screen reader. Making accessible tables can be especially difficult for educators as accessibility checkers don't always indicate all the steps needed to make a table fully accessible. Avoiding the use of unnecessary tables can be an easy way to create more accessible content for students using a screen reader while also making course content more visually appealing for students using a mobile device.

To ensure that the layout of a page looks visually appealing on a mobile device or on a laptop, we also want to make sure that we use responsive images (Baldwin & Ching, 2020). Responsive images adjust to the size of the screen, so if I view a page with a responsive image on a laptop, it will fill the screen. If I view the image on a mobile device, it will adjust to the size of my phone screen. Using responsive images is a double-duty strategy that not only helps to create an aesthetic learning experience for students regardless of the device they are using, but it is also helpful to create an accessible course as it ensures no images are too small to be easily viewed by students with visual disabilities.

Removing additional downloads or taps/clicks is another step we can take to help create visually appealing pages. One way we can remove additional downloads or taps/clicks is to move content, when possible, directly into the LMS. Many LMSs have an app version so students can access the LMS easily on their mobile device. By moving content directly into a LMS's pages instead of having students download a Word document or PDF, we can make use of an app that has already been optimized for use with a mobile device (Seilhamer et al., 2020). This is also a double-duty strategy as it removes the additional step of having to check a Word document or PDF for accessibility. When we move the content of that Word document or PDF directly into a page on our LMS, we can use the built-in accessibility checker in the LMS to ensure we haven't skipped any headers and verify that alternative text is added to images.

Using descriptive links instead of a full URL is another double-duty strategy that allows us to create a visually appealing page on a mobile device (Baldwin & Ching, 2020) while creating accessible course content.

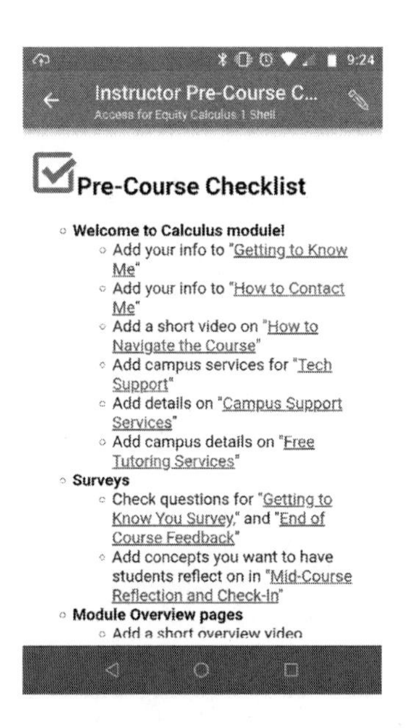

Figure 3.4 View of a pre-course checklist with descriptive hyperlinks on a mobile device.

A descriptive hyperlink means that instead of simply copying and pasting https://www.pewresearch.org/internet/fact-sheet/mobile/ to the page we will highlight Pew Research Center and add the link so it appears like this: Pew Research Center. For students using screen readers, this means that they won't have to listen to a screen reader reading the entire (often meaningless) URL (WebAIM, 2022). Now let's take a moment and see how the use of descriptive links contrasts with the use of full URLs on a mobile device. Figure 3.4 shows a page viewed on a mobile device with descriptive hyperlinks. Contrast this page to Figure 3.5, which shows the exact same page, but with full URLs (Box 3.2).

You may have noticed that the page with the full URLs became much longer. When I used the full URLs instead of descriptive links, the same content could no longer fit on my small screen. I would have to scroll to be able to see the same information that fit on my phone screen when I used descriptive hyperlinks. In this way, we can see in action how using a descriptive hyperlink is an important strategy for minimizing the limitation of a small screen.

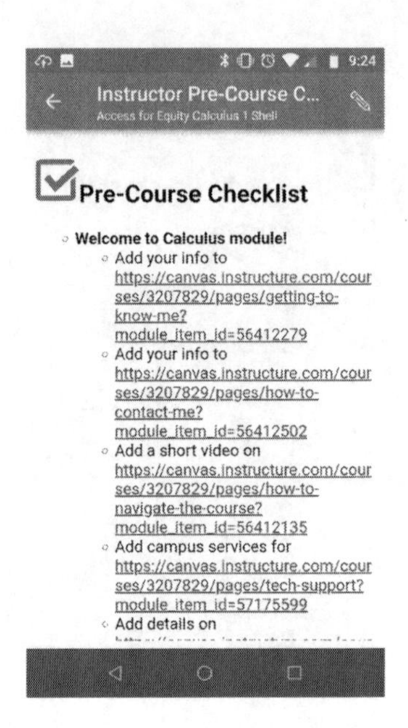

Figure 3.5 View of a pre-course checklist with full URLS on a mobile device.

BOX 3.2 REFLECTION

Now let's take a moment to reflect on the student experience viewing these pages on a mobile device. What stands out to you as a difference between Figure 3.4 and Figure 3.5?

There are also easy steps we can take when typing the content of our pages in a LMS to make a page more visually appealing on a small screen. For example, using 14-point font and a consistent sans serif typeface (e.g., Open Sans) can help make a page easier to read for students using a mobile device (Baldwin & Ching, 2020). This also helps to create a page that is accessible to students with visual disabilities who benefit from a slightly larger typeface and a simple, consistent font (WebAIM, 2020). In addition, indenting content infrequently is important when designing for a small screen (Baldwin & Ching, 2020). Finally, using bold for emphasis can help create a page that is easier to read on a mobile device (Baldwin & Ching, 2020) and can help support reading performance for students with dyslexia when compared to the use of italics for emphasis (Rello & Baeza-Yates, 2013).

Each of the strategies presented in this section help to create a visually appealing experience for students using a mobile device to access course content. These strategies are also commonly cited ways to make a course accessible to students with disabilities. By being mindful of these double-duty strategies, we can take important strides to create a course that serves every student in our course whether they are using a mobile device or a screen reader.

Transforming the limitation of small screens into a benefit

In this chapter, we explored strategies we may already be using to create accessible courses for students with disabilities. These strategies allow us to create courses specifically designed for small screens and are as follows (Box 3.3):

BOX 3.3 MOBILE DESIGN IN ACTION

CREATE CONTENT FOR SMALL SCREENS

- Chunking Content
  - Use modules to organize course content
  - Add text headers to modules
  - Add headers to pages
  - Use accordions or tabs
- Creating a Visually Appealing and Accessible Experience
  - Avoid tables
  - Use responsive images
  - Move content directly into the LMS
  - Use descriptive hyperlinks
  - Use Sans Serif fonts and 14-point font
  - Avoid indenting
  - Use bold (not italics) for emphasis

By making these strategies part of our workflow when creating modules and pages in our LMS, we can create a welcoming and inclusive environment that is designed to serve all our students (Box 3.4).

BOX 3.4 REFLECTION

Now let's take a moment to reflect on these strategies. Which of these strategies are already part of your practice? Which of these strategies do you commit to making part of your practice when designing content for students? Take a moment to set an intention to choose one or two strategies that you will begin implementing tomorrow. Taking steps to implement more of these strategies can have a big impact on how students experience course content on mobile devices.

These double-duty strategies help us to minimize the limitation of small screens by chunking content and designing visually appealing pages that translate well onto a mobile device. When considering cognitive load, these strategies even allow us to transform the limitation of a small screen into a benefit by helping students to focus on one task at a time (Eschenbrenner & Nah, 2019). By designing course content that translates well onto a mobile device, we can create a learning experience in which students can move fluidly between a laptop, computer, tablet, or smartphone without suffering the irritation of viewing content designed for a laptop on the small screen of a mobile device.

References

Baldwin, S.J., & Ching, Y.H. (2020). Guidelines for designing online courses for mobile devices. *TechTrends*, *64*(3), 413–422.

Eschenbrenner, B., & Nah, F.F.H. (2019). Learning through mobile devices: Leveraging affordances as facilitators of engagement. *International Journal of Mobile Learning and Organisation*, *13*(2), 152–170. 10.1504/ijmlo.2019.098193

Major, A., & Calandrino, T. (2018). Beyond chunking: Micro-learning secrets for effective online design. *FDLA Journal*, *3*(1), 13.

Méndez-Carbajo, D., & Wolla, S.A. (2019). Segmenting educational content: Long-form vs. short-form online learning modules. *American Journal of Distance Education*, *33*(2), 108–119. 10.1080/08923647.2019.1583514

Miller, C. (2011). Aesthetics and e-assessment: The interplay of emotional design and learner performance. *Distance Education*, *32*(3), 307–337. 10.1080/01587919.2011.610291

Rello, L., & Baeza-Yates, R. (2013). Good fonts for dyslexia. Proceedings of *the 15th International ACM SIGACCESS Conference on Computers and Accessibility*. 1–8.

Seilhamer, R., Johnson, D., Keefe, E., & Philips, L. (2020). Course evaluation checklist: Mobile app design considerations. Canvas. https://community.canvaslms.com/t5/Canvas-Instructional-Designer/Mobile-App-Design-Course-Evaluation-Checklist/ba-p/276877

Web Accessibility Initiative (2022a). *Keep text succinct*. Web Accessibility Initiative. https://www.w3.org/WAI/WCAG2/supplemental/patterns/o3p05-succinct-text/

Web Accessibility Initiative. (2022b). *Accordion (Sections With Show/Hide Functionality)*. Web Accessibility Initiative. https://www.w3.org/WAI/ARIA/apg/patterns/accordion/

WebAIM. (2018, February 9). *Creating accessible tables*. Web Accessibility in Mind. https://webaim.org/techniques/tables/

WebAIM. (2020, October 27). *Typefaces and fonts*. Web Accessibility in Mind. https://webaim.org/techniques/fonts/

WebAIM. (2022). *Links and hypertext*. Web Accessibility in Mind. https://webaim.org/techniques/hypertext/link_text

4

BUILD TRUST

CARE, UNDERSTANDING, AND ACCEPTANCE BY DESIGN

The power of relationships

In my first year of teaching ninth-grade English, I attended our weekly whole-school meeting with the Vice Principals and Principal. One of the Vice Principals gave a short presentation on a school-wide focus we would explore in the new school year: relationships. As a new teacher, I was sitting on the edge of my seat … I was so excited to see an intentional focus on the power of building meaningful relationships in our classrooms. The Vice Principal shared strategies such as storytelling of our own experiences as students, welcoming students at the door, and getting to know our students. Throughout my teaching career, I have seen first-hand the power of relationships. Whether I was teaching ninth-grade English, first-year college composition, work experience, or online education pedagogy to faculty, the most meaningful, goose-bump inducing moments of my career have been because of positive and meaningful relationships with students. I have worked with students who

DOI: 10.4324/9781003328773-6

have persisted through tremendous changes and challenges in their personal lives, such as the birth of a child, car accidents, and illness. Through the relationship we built, we were able to work together to ensure they had the flexibility they needed to attend to their personal lives while still maintaining progress towards their degree.

As educators, we have likely experienced the transformative power relationships can have on the learning experience. Research supports our experience and shows strong instructor–student relationships have a powerful impact on student learning (Cung et al., 2018; Sher, 2009), satisfaction (Sher, 2009), and retention (Mitchell & Hughes, 2014). As with any relationship, trust is an essential component of strong instructor–student relationships.

Building relationships through trust

Though there is a limited amount of research that focuses specifically on trust in higher education (Cavanagh et al., 2018; Payne et al., 2022), trust emerges again and again as a key component of positive instructor–student relationships (Cavanagh, 2018; Hagenauer & Volet, 2014). Payne et al. (2022) explained *trust* as a "relational practice that enables growth, recognition, empowerment, community, and possibility" (p. 9). According to this definition of *trust*, the impacts of trust in teacher–student relationships have a profound impact on not only the student's experience in a course, but also on the student's life. By building trust with students, we can foster a truly transformative educational experience. As educators, our jobs really are to make dreams come true and change lives. However, the life-changing, soul-fulfilling potential of education cannot be realized without trust between educators and students.

Trust is at once both profound and minute. Although trust has a big impact on student engagement and performance (Cavanagh et al., 2018), we often build trust with others in the smallest ways (Brown, 2015). Trust between educators and students can be defined as "a perception that the instructor understands the challenges facing students as they progress through the course, accepts students for who they are, and cares about the educational welfare of students" (Cavanagh et al., 2018, p. 2). As educators, small moves that we make can have outsized impacts on building trust and communicating to our students understanding, acceptance, and care (Box 4.1).

BOX 4.1 REFLECTION

Now let's take a moment and reflect on small moves that have built trust with your students in big ways.

Reflecting on my own teaching, I am struck with how small moves on my part have had a profound impact on the trust I was able to build with students. For example, after a student told me a parent was experiencing health troubles, I asked about their parent a week later. Although this move took little time on my part, this small gesture had profound impact on the trust I was able to build with this student and helped the student know I truly cared.

As educators, we can build student trust through small practices such as knowing (and using) student names, providing feedback, being transparent, explaining the reason behind learning activities, demonstrating acceptance, recognizing challenges students face, and creating a consistent learning experience (Cavanagh et al., 2018). Another way we can build trust with students is through mobile-friendly course design. Mobile-friendly course design can be an especially effective way of building trust with students. Cavanagh et al. (2018) noted the importance of "establishing trust early and often" (p. 2). By leveraging mobile-friendly course design strategies, we can help to build trust with students from the moment they first log into our course.

Mobile design principle #2: Build trust

The design of our courses within a LMS can help build trust even before the first day of class as students often log in to the LMS before the semester begins. For students in online or hybrid courses, building trust through design is especially critical as other trust-building moments such as kind welcomes at the door and quick thank-yous for asking questions after class are not possible. In these instances, intentionally designing a course that builds trust and creates a welcoming and inclusive environment is essential for supporting student learning.

To build trust through design we can focus on three overarching approaches: showing care through consistency, demonstrating acceptance by removing wait times, and communicating acceptance by designing for touch screens. The following sections will explore specific strategies we can use to enact each of these approaches to create mobile-friendly course content and build trust.

Showing care through consistency

As educators, we can show care for students by creating a consistent learning experience. Consistency demonstrates care as it shows empathy for the student experience and helps to remove a sense of discomfort that students may feel when they don't know what is going to happen in the course next week. Consistency is a powerful tool for building trust with anyone and especially our students as it helps to support a sense of reliability. Brown's (2015) framework, the anatomy of trust, highlights the importance of reliability for building trust. In relationships, reliability means that I stick to what I say I am going to do. In our personal lives, we see first-hand the importance of reliability. For example, if I tell my daughter I am going to make her lunch, I will make her lunch. In our personal relationships, we experience the importance of reliability for establishing and maintaining trust.

Reliability is just as important in the classroom as it is in our relationships with our children, our spouses, and our friends. We can build trust with our students by demonstrating reliability through consistency. For example, instead of having weekly assignments due at differing days throughout the semester, we can help create a sense of consistency by having weekly assignments due the same day each week (e.g., discussion posts are always due on Mondays). There are also key design strategies that we can use to create a sense of consistency for students that help to build trust while also creating mobile-friendly course content.

One of the most important design strategies we can use to create mobile-friendly course content and build trust is to keep navigation simplified, consistent, and clear (Baldwin & Ching, 2020). We can do this by keeping navigation options limited so students are not bombarded by too many options. LMSs will sometimes include default pages in the course navigation menus that don't apply to a course. For example, in my own practice site in Canvas there are 17 items that show up by default in

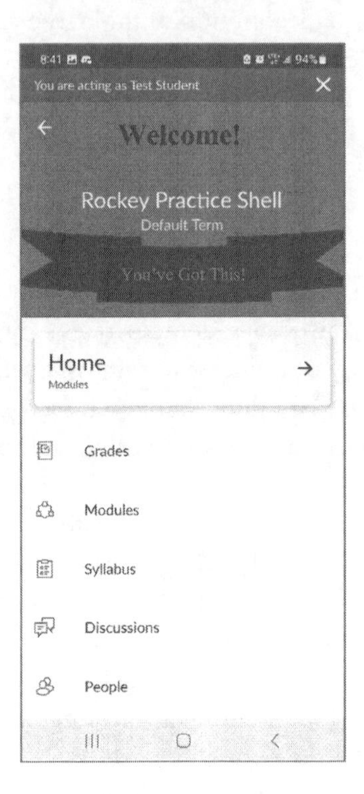

Figure 4.1 Students cannot view all the navigation options without scrolling on a mobile device.

the course navigation. Figure 4.1 shows an example of the default course navigation. Of course, the 17 items don't fit on my phone screen, so as a student I have to scroll quite a bit to see all the options.

Figure 4.2 in contrast shows a simplified menu. In this case, the entire menu fits on the small screen of my phone. This simplified course menu makes the course easier to navigate on a mobile device, but it also benefits all students as it helps to prevent students from getting lost in pages that aren't used.

After we have designed a simplified navigation menu, we can focus on creating a sense of consistency in the navigation of a course. This helps to build trust with students as they know exactly what to expect in our courses each week. One helpful strategy for keeping navigation consistent is to use the same organization each week. For example, in each module, I could include an overview, course content, and assignments. Whether it

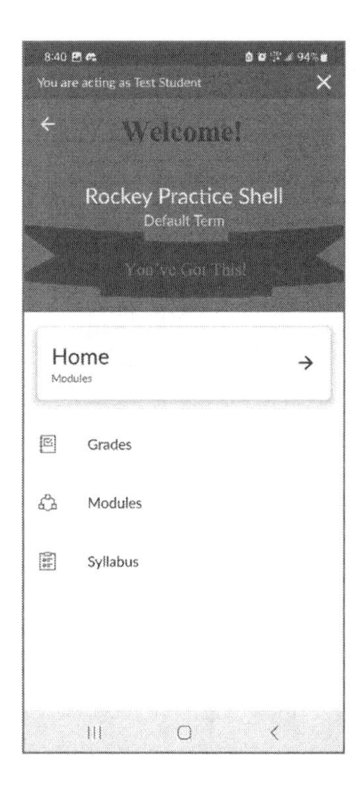

Figure 4.2 A simplified navigation allows students to view all course navigation options without having to scroll.

is week 1 or week 10, students will know to expect an overview, course content, and assignments.

Finally, once we have ensured navigation is simplified and consistent, we can create clarity around navigation by communicating to students how to navigate the course. We can do this by recording a short 2–5 minute video where we share our screen while we walk students through how to navigate the course and what to expect in each module (Baldwin & Ching, 2020). This short video can be a powerful opportunity to show care for our students and highlight the consistency between modules. It can also be an opportunity for us to guide students on how to navigate the course on their phones.

Consistency can be a powerful way to show we care and to build trust with our students. Making the navigation of our course simplified, consistent, and clear makes a powerful first impression and helps to create a sense of consistency for students as they navigate our courses. When we're designing course content on LMSs, we need to be considerate of the student experience. An LMS can help to connect students to our course beyond the confines of a wall and (when mobile-design strategies are leveraged) beyond the confines of a computer screen. However, it can also create an additional space that students need to learn how to navigate. Inconsistent course navigation can make students feel like they are trying to find a classroom that moves to a different location on campus each week. When students are using mobile devices, this makes it even more difficult. A small screen on a mobile device makes it harder to see the big picture. It can feel like trying to find a classroom when you can only see two feet in front of you at a time.

Demonstrating understanding by removing wait times

As educators, we can demonstrate an understanding of the student experience on a mobile device by trying to remove wait times. Although smartphone ownership is nearly ubiquitous for 18- to 29-year-olds (Pew Research Center, 2021), students may be using older devices that are slower. If anyone has used an older phone or has tried to load a page when the service is spotty, they will understand first-hand the importance of removing wait times for students accessing courses on a mobile device (Box 4.2).

BOX 4.2 REFLECTION

Now let's take a moment to think about a time you have tried to access a website on a mobile device that was slow to load. What did you do? How did you feel? How did the loading time of the website impact your experience and actions?

I'm guessing that many of us have abandoned a task on a mobile device when the page loaded too slowly. We're not alone in this. Adams et al. (2015) noted that if a website takes too long to load on a mobile device, 29% of users will immediately switch to a different website and 40% of shoppers will leave a page if it takes more than three seconds to load. Although students may not have a choice to switch to a different website when working on coursework, wait times can be incredibly frustrating for them.

One way we can remove wait times is to avoid requiring students to download documents (Asiimwe & Grönlund, 2015). Downloading files on a mobile device can be difficult, especially when the files are large (Asiimwe & Grönlund, 2015). One way we can limit downloads in our courses is to move content directly into the LMS when possible. As mentioned in Chapter 3, this can help make it easier to check for accessibility as we can use built-in accessibility checkers in the LMS. It also helps to remove wait times for students using mobile devices. If we do need to share a file for students to download (e.g., a PowerPoint for students to take lecture notes), saving the file as a PDF allows the file to be easily downloaded whether a student is using an Android device or an iPhone (Farley et al., 2015).

We can also make courses load faster on mobile devices by limiting unnecessary images (Baldwin & Ching, 2020). This strategy helps to mitigate the limitation of small screens when we remove visual clutter caused by unnecessary images. If we do have an image that is necessary to include, we can help remove wait times by being mindful of the file size. The days of dial-up and waiting for our computers to connect to the internet are behind us. Today, people expect instantaneous access to the internet and fast load times (Adams et al., 2015). Using smaller-sized images can be a helpful way to speed up load time for course content.

Finally, we can help to remove wait times by limiting unnecessary clicks. Each additional click required of students increases the amount of time it takes for a student to begin to complete a task. By reducing the number of clicks, we can help students get to our course content faster and with less stress (Rios et al., 2018).

Each of these strategies provides an opportunity for us to show students we understand what it is like to navigate a course on a mobile device. By being mindful of the student experience on a mobile device, we can remove the stress of wait times and create a more pleasant experience for all students, including those who are accessing a course on a mobile device.

Communicating acceptance by designing for touch screens

Although many of our students use phones frequently in their personal lives, they may feel guilt or shame for using their phones for coursework.

Some students may have internalized bans on mobile devices that continue to persist in K–12 classes (National Center for Education Statistics, 2021). Other students may feel that they should have access to reliable home internet or a fast laptop. Still other students may feel that they really aren't supposed to use phones for academic purposes. As Barden and Bygroves (2017) noted in their case study, it was more comfortable for a student to pretend to text in class than to have the instructor become aware that they were using their phone for learning purposes. However, as discussed in Chapter 1, leveraging mobile devices for learning can remove barriers of access for students. For many students, being able to use their phone to access coursework and complete assignments can mean the difference between passing or failing a course.

As educators, we know that it is not enough to remove barriers; we need to actively communicate to students that these barriers have been broken down. Estrada et al. (2018) explored the power of "kindness cues" for students. Kindness cues, defined as "micro cues affirming social inclusion and respect for dignity," can support student success and persistence (Estrada et al., 2018, p. 4).

By demonstrating acceptance of students' use of phones for learning, we can create a course that intentionally sends kindness cues to students that their use of mobile devices for learning is welcome and supported.

When we are designing our course content, we can think of moves that we make to create mobile-friendly course content as ways to send our students kindness cues. These kindness cues make it clear to students that their use of mobile devices for learning is appropriate and respected. One strategy is to create directions that work regardless of device (Baldwin & Ching, 2020). For example, instead of saying "click submit" we can simply say "tap or click submit." This small change can signal to students that we accept their use of mobile devices for learning.

Embedding videos directly into a page can also demonstrate acceptance by designing for touch screens on mobile devices. By embedding videos directly onto a page instead of providing a link to the video, students can tap or click on the video without even having to leave the page. Embedding videos directly into an LMS page benefits students using computers as well as students using mobile devices as it eliminates extra clicks and helps prevent students from getting lost (as easily) down a YouTube rabbit hole.

We can also design for touch screens by hyperlinking email addresses and phone numbers (Baldwin & Ching, 2020). In doing so, students can simply tap a phone number to make a call and/or tap an email address to begin sending us an email. In this way, we can not only leverage touch screens, but also make it easier for students to reach out to us (or important student resources on campus) with just one tap. To create a hyperlinked email address, simply select the email and add the hyperlink "mailto:email address." A phone number can be hyperlinked by selecting the phone number and adding the link "tel:phonenumber."

By designing for touch screens, we can demonstrate acceptance for students using mobile devices to access course content. Creating a course that is designed to be easy to use with a touch screen (or a computer) can help us to send our students kindness cues (Estrada et al., 2018) and create a course that is welcoming and inclusive from the first tap.

Trust by design

Building trust with students is foundational to our work as educators. Although trust a has big impact on student performance and engagement (Cavanagh et al., 2018), we often build trust with students in small ways (Brown, 2015). This chapter explored ways in which we can make small moves to show care through consistency, demonstrate understanding by removing wait times, and communicate acceptance by designing for touch screens (Box 4.3).

BOX 4.3 MOBILE DESIGN IN ACTION

BUILD TRUST

- Showing Care through Consistency
    - Simplify navigation
    - Keep navigation consistent
    - Ensure navigation is clear

- Demonstrating Understanding by Removing Wait Times
  - Avoid requiring students to download files
  - Remove unnecessary images
  - Be mindful of file sizes of images
  - Limit unnecessary clicks
- Communicating Acceptance by Designing for Touch Screens
  - Create directions that work regardless of device
  - Embed videos directly into the page
  - Hyperlink email addresses and phone numbers

Each of these strategies for mobile-friendly course design provide an opportunity to build trust by design (Box 4.4).

BOX 4.4 REFLECTION

Now let's take a moment to reflect on these strategies. Which of these strategies are already part of your practice? Which of these strategies do you commit to making part of your practice when designing content for students? Take a moment to set an intention to choose one or two strategies that you will begin implementing tomorrow. Taking steps to implement more of these strategies can have a big impact on how students experience course content on mobile devices.

Mobile-friendly course design presents an opportunity to build trust with students from the moment they first log in to our course. These strategies will help to build trust with all students regardless of which device they use. They will also work to show care, demonstrate understanding, and communicate acceptance to students who are using their phones to access course content. As many students may feel a sense of shame for using their phones to access course content, an important piece of mobile-friendly course design is creating a course that sends cues to students that phones are helpful tools to use for learning. Small moves like saying "tap or click" instead of just "click" can go a long way towards empowering students to leverage the tools they already carry in their pockets to be successful in our courses.

References

Adams, L., Burkholder, E., Hamilton, K. (2015). Micro-moments: Your guide to winning the shift to mobile. Google. https://www.thinkwithgoogle.com/_qs/documents/34/micromoments-guide-to-winning-shift-to-mobile-download.pdf

Asiimwe, E., & Grönlund, Å. (2015). MLCMS actual use, perceived use, and experiences of use. *International Journal of Education and Development Using ICT*, *11*(1), 101–121.

Baldwin, S.J., & Ching, Y.H. (2020). Guidelines for designing online courses for mobile devices. *TechTrends*, *64*(3), 413–422.

Barden, O., & Bygroves, M. (2017). 'I wouldn't be able to graduate if it wasn't for my mobile phone.' The affordances of mobile devices in the construction of complex academic texts. *Innovations in Education and Teaching International*, *55*, 555–565. 10.1080/14703297.2017.1322996

Brown, B. (2015). *Supersoul Sessions: The Anatomy of Trust* [Video]. https://brenebrown.com/videos/anatomy-trust-video/

Cavanagh, A.J., Chen, X., Bathgate, M., Frederick, J., Hanauer, D.I., & Graham, M.J. (2018). Trust, growth mindset, and student commitment to active learning in a college science course. *CBE—Life Sciences Education*, *17*(1). 10.1187/cbe.17-06-0107

Cung, B., Xu, D., & Eichhorn, S. (2018). Increasing interpersonal interactions in an online course: Does increased instructor email activity and voluntary meeting time in a physical classroom facilitate student learning?. *Online Learning*, *22*(3), 193–215.

Estrada, M., Eroy-Reveles, A., & Matsui, J. (2018). The influence of affirming kindness and community on broadening participation in STEM career pathways. *Social Issues and Policy Review*, *12*(1), 258. 10.1111/sipr.12046

Farley, H., Murphy, A., Johnson, C., Carter, B., Lane, M., Midgley, W., Hafeez-Baig, A., Dekeyser, S., & Koronios, A. (2015). How do students use their mobile devices to support learning? A case study from an Australian regional university. *Journal of Interactive Media in Education*, *2015*(1). 1-13. 10.5334/jime.ar

Hagenauer, G., & Volet, S.E. (2014). Teacher–student relationship at university: An important yet under-researched field, *Oxford Review of Education*, *40*(3), 370–388, 10.1080/03054985.2014.921613

Mitchell, Y.F., & Hughes, G.D. (2014). Demographic and instructor-student interaction factors associated with community college students' intent to persist. *Journal of Research in Education*, *24*(2), 63–78.

National Center for Education Statistics. (2021, October). *School Survey on Crime and Safety*. https://nces.ed.gov/programs/digest/d21/tables/dt21_233.50.asp

Payne, A.L., Stone, C., & Bennett, R. (2022). Conceptualising and building trust to enhance the engagement and achievement of under-served students. *The Journal of Continuing Higher Education*, 1–18. 10.1080/07377363.2021.2005759

Pew Research Center (2021). Mobile fact sheet. https://www.pewresearch.org/internet/fact-sheet/mobile/

Rios, T., Elliott, M., & Mandernach, B.J. (2018). Efficient instructional strategies for maximizing online student satisfaction. *Journal of Educators Online*, *15*(3).

Sher, A. (2009). Assessing the relationship of student-instructor and student-student interaction to student learning and satisfaction in web-based online learning environment. *Journal of Interactive Online Learning*, *8*(2),102–120.

5

LEVERAGE MOMENTS

FILLING THE IN-BETWEEN PARTS OF A DAY

Designing for anytime/anywhere learning: Reflecting on students' use of mobile devices

I went back to work when my daughter was six weeks old. Not wanting to start my daughter in daycare yet, I jigsawed my mom's schedule, my work schedule, and my husband's schedule so one of the three of us could care for her. At the time, my husband was in the third year of his PhD. He was also teaching as an adjunct at a community college and working as a teaching assistant at the University of California, Davis. His commute to either campus ranged from 40 minutes to an hour and a half. Our schedule was jampacked and constantly shifting. As a grad student, my husband didn't have much control over his schedule and had to, at times, make last-minute changes to attend lectures or collect data. Sometimes this meant I started my work in the early hours of the morning before the gates to my office even opened. As a new mom, I did not hesitate to climb the gate to get into my office to start my workday so I could get back to my daughter.

DOI: 10.4324/9781003328773-7

Eight months later, I started my PhD program. As two graduate students balancing childcare and multiple jobs, all we had were the in-between moments of our day. I would find time to read academic articles while I was commuting to campus via multiple buses. My husband studied for his qualifying exams while my daughter napped next to him. These in-between moments allowed us to be there for our daughter while also making consistent progress toward our degrees.

Making strategic use of these in-between moments of our day for work and learning can help us to maximize the precious extended periods of time in our day for focus-intensive projects. Moore (2020) noted the power of these "small moments" for persisting in times of disruption (e.g., a global pandemic) and helping to better set ourselves up to make use of the precious times that we have an hour or more to devote to a task. Even now, when I'm largely working on campus and have long since earned my PhD, my phone allows me to make use of the in-between times in my day. When I'm waiting to pick my daughter up from school, I can use my phone to read articles I rarely can dig into on days filled with meetings and emails.

These in-between parts of the day hold tremendous potential for supporting student learning for two reasons. First, many of our students are balancing childcare, elder care, long commutes, and/or demanding work schedules. When we create mobile-friendly course content, students can make use of the in-between moments of their day to read an article for our class or contribute to a course discussion. Second, these in-between moments of the day provide an opportunity for students to realize the potential of mobile devices to support anytime/anywhere learning. By providing students the opportunity to use their phones to learn anytime and anywhere, we can support student learning by creating courses students engage with more frequently.

Mobile design principle #3: Leverage moments

Research suggests that students use mobile devices for shorter periods of time (López & Silva, 2014; Seilhamer et al., 2018) and to fill the in-between parts of a day (Farley et al., 2015). To effectively create mobile-friendly courses, we need to create course content that aligns with how students already use their phones for learning. Designing course content that would require students to use their phone for extended periods of time would be like requiring a chef to use a grill to boil eggs. I'm no chef, but while I could technically boil eggs on a grill, I prefer to use my grill for burgers. Whatever technology we're using, whether it be a grill or a smartphone, it helps to design experiences around ways in which people already use that technology. By creating course content that is designed to be worked through in smaller chunks of time and also lets students fill the in-between moments of their day, we can amplify how students are already using mobile devices to truly leverage this tool to support anytime/anywhere learning (Ally, 2013; Barden & Bygroves, 2018).

Creating content in ten-minute chunks

Chunking content into short segments can help our courses align with how students already use their mobile devices. Students typically use mobile devices for shorter tasks and computers for longer, more in-depth tasks (López & Silva, 2014; Seilhamer et al., 2018). In my focus group on mobile device usage in STEM courses, one student noted, "If it's like a little ten-minute thing, the phone's great because it's easy. You don't have to pull it out. You don't have to, you know, login and connect to the internet, all that kind of stuff." For students, the convenience of a mobile device means that they will often use their phones for shorter periods of time, but more frequently throughout the day. Andrews et al. (2015) noted that participants used phones an average of approximately 85 times a day and on average spent five hours on a phone. Interestingly, 55% of phone uses lasted for less than 30 seconds (Andrews et al., 2015). Designing "easy, low-stake tasks" (Baldwin & Ching, 2020, p. 413) that take less than ten minutes can be a powerful way to align the design of our course with how students already use mobile devices.

As educators, we can chunk content in ten-minute increments to align with how students use mobile devices to support the benefits of anytime/anywhere learning (Ally, 2013; Barden & Bygroves, 2018). In Chapter 3, we explored strategies for chunking content to minimize the limitation of small screens. Those strategies (using modules, adding headers, and using tabs) can help to chunk content into smaller chunks. In addition, we can also strive to keep pages around 2,000 words or less (Baldwin & Ching, 2020).

After chunking content into ten-minute chunks, we can consider strategies for designing course content in which students can easily pick up where they left off. These strategies can help students to make steady progress on our courses in the in-between moments of their day.

Designing for stops and starts

After we have chunked course content into ten-minute chunks (or less), we can focus on designing course content so students can easily pick up where they left off. Even at resident four-year institutions, the so-called traditional student who has no responsibilities outside of coursework is not the norm (Aslanian & Clinefelter, 2012). Students today are often balancing long commutes, multiple jobs, childcare, elder care, and/or sibling care. For students balancing multiple demands on their time, it may be difficult to find long chunks of uninterrupted time to work through course content.

Imagine a student mother with a three-year-old and a seven-year-old and a part-time job. She may have ten minutes to read an article before she wakes up her kids for school. Then, after dropping off her kids at school, she may find another seven minutes before she clocks in at work where she can listen to a chunk of a lecture podcast. After that, she may find another ten minutes to complete a getting-to-know-you survey during a break at work. Chunking content in this way allows the course to fit into her day instead of her having to try to find a solid chunk of time to work on the course.

When students can work on coursework throughout the day it supports a flexibility that many students need to succeed. Being able to work on a course throughout the day also supports student learning. Research suggests that the more students interact with course content, the more successful they are in a course (Murray et al., 2012; Zimmerman, 2012) As educators, we know that the more frequently students interact with course content, the more they will be able to retain in the long-term. Chunking content to create mobile-friendly courses provides an opportunity for educators to encourage the opposite of cramming.

The first step to design for these starts and stops is to create a consistent way to communicate to students when pages are especially suited for completion on a mobile device. Many students may have internalized a sense of shame for using mobile devices for learning given continued bans on mobile devices (National Center for Education Statistics, 2021). Students may feel that mobile devices are only to be used for off-task behavior, not for learning (Barden & Bygroves, 2018). As such, we as educators need to communicate to students how and when they can use mobile devices for learning. For example, we could add a short page to an introduction module that explains how students can use their mobile devices to be successful in our course and when they can use mobile devices. As we are designing mobile-friendly courses on a continuum, there may be components of our courses that are better suited for mobile devices. If there is course content that requires a computer, we can communicate this to students with a short symbol (with the appropriate alt text) indicating that that page will require a computer. We can also indicate the pages that are mobile-friendly by adding an image of a mobile device.

After we communicate with students how and when they can use mobile devices for our course, we want to ensure that students have strategies to minimize the distractibility factor of mobile devices. We can't effectively leverage moments for learning if we are constantly distracted. As discussed in Chapter 2, mobile devices can have a powerful pull on our attention. We need to support students in learning how to manage the pull of their mobile devices. One strategy for managing the attention-pulling aspect of mobile devices is to be mindful about how we have set notifications. I have found that managing notifications of apps has been essential for my professional and personal life. For example, when I am writing or working on tasks that require deep concentration, I turn my phone on "Do Not Disturb" and set the exception that calls from my daughter's school will go through. My husband, my mom, and my best friend know that if they really need to get a hold of me, they may need to call twice to bypass "Do Not Disturb". For my personal life, I turn on my "Do Not Disturb" and put my phone in the other room in the evenings so my daughter and I can watch *Full House* uninterrupted. Without these strategies, it would be too easy to get distracted by the dings from my phone when I get an email or when someone likes something on Twitter.

Learning to set notifications to manage my personal and professional life took time (and, of course, failure). After getting distracted by Twitter one too many times during my focused writing time, I needed to come up with a solution. Students may also need guidance on how to set notifications. We can include this guidance when we explain how to use mobile devices to support learning in our courses. Students will most likely want to set notifications so that they can receive messages from us about the course, but they'll want to silence notifications from social media when they are watching a lecture video or listening to a podcast lecture on their phone. Setting notifications is essential to support students in making the most of a ten-minute chunk in their day. When we are uninterrupted, it is amazing what we can accomplish in ten minutes.

To create course content students can work through in the in-between parts of the day, we also need to gain a deeper understanding of how students already use their phones for learning. Although research suggests students typically use their phones for shorter tasks (López & Silva, 2014; Seilhamer et al., 2018), you may have noticed specific ways students tend to use your institution's LMS on their phone for learning (Box 5.1).

BOX 5.1 REFLECTION

Take a moment and reflect on how students use the LMS on their phones. Are there pages students consistently seem to miss? Are there pages students always seem to complete?

Upon reflection, we may find that we have noticed common trends in how students navigate an LMS on their phones. For example, many instructors on my campus know that students tend to navigate Canvas by looking at the "To Dos." The "To Dos" are also easily visible when you first open the Canvas Student app, as shown in Figure 5.1.

This can be helpful for students to easily see what assignments are due in all their courses. However, when students only look at the "To Dos" they may miss important content in the module that will help prepare them for an assignment. As an educator, understanding how students navigate my course can help me to design course content that leverages moments and aligns with how students navigate the LMS on their phone. For example, in Canvas, I may decide to add requirements to certain

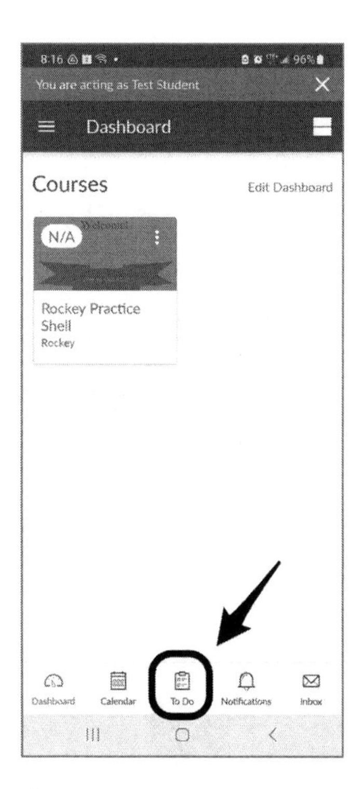

Figure 5.1 Student view of Canvas when opening the student app on a phone.

pages within a module so that students need to view those pages before completing an assignment. For students, when they access the "To Dos" they will be prompted to finish the module requirements to unlock a particular assignment.

To get a sense of how students use the LMS on their phone, we could survey students. We could also ask a few students to walk us through how they use their phones to work through course content on their mobile device.

Finally, we can help students easily pick up where they left off in our course by using features of our LMS that indicate when a student has completed an activity. LMSs may have a feature in which the instructor can require students to view something or submit something. In Canvas, this feature is called "requirements" in modules. In Moodle, this feature is referred to as "Activity Completion." Figure 5.2 shows a student view of requirements added to a module in Canvas.

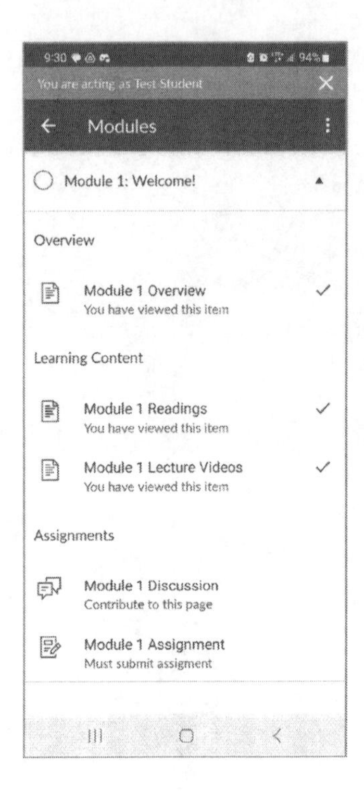

Figure 5.2 Using requirements in Canvas allows students to easily pick up where they left off.

Leveraging this feature of Canvas allows students to easily pick up where they left off. When I look at Module 1 in Figure 5.2, I can see that I have viewed the overview page, readings, and lecture videos. I also know that I still need to complete the discussion and the assignment. Once I fully complete the module, I will see a check mark in the white bubble next to "Module 1." These check marks can help support students who are using a mobile device to access course content in the in-between parts of the day as they can easily pick up where they left off. Students won't need to waste time trying to figure out where they left off.

Designing for stops and starts creates an opportunity for students to fill the in-between parts of their day with our coursework. The strategies presented in this section help to support students who are balancing multiple demands on their time, including childcare, long commutes, sibling care, elder care, and/or work obligations. These strategies also benefit all students, as being able to interact with course content frequently in smaller chunks throughout the day supports student learning.

Expanding access in ten-minute chunks

Students may choose to use a mobile device for quicker tasks and a computer to work through tasks that require longer and more in-depth concentration. Although creating course content that aligns with student use of mobile devices for quick tasks supports all students, it is a design move that benefits students who are balancing childcare, work, and/or long commutes. Many of our students have multiple demands on their time, but the in-between parts of their day offer important opportunities to make progress on coursework. In this chapter, we explored the following strategies to create content in ten-minute chunks and design for stops and starts (Box 5.2).

BOX 5.2 MOBILE DESIGN IN ACTION

LEVERAGE MOMENTS

- Creating Content in Ten-Minute Chunks
  - Chunk content into quick tasks
  - Keep pages short (less than 2,000 words)
- Designing for Stops and Starts
  - Create a consistent way to communicate mobile-friendly course content
  - Encourage students to turn on some notifications and turn off others
  - Design for how students use the LMS on their phone
  - Add completion requirements

Imagine if instead of scrolling absently through TikTok students could use the five minutes waiting in line at the grocery store to read a short article. Then later, while they cook dinner, they could have a lecture podcast playing to review a difficult concept. All students benefit from the ability to fill the in-between parts of their day with coursework, but these strategies can transform the learning experience for students who are juggling multiple demands on their time and responsibilities. By designing course content for how students already use mobile devices, we can leverage smartphones to expand access to our course (Box 5.3).

BOX 5.3 REFLECTION

Now let's take a moment to reflect on these strategies. Which of these strategies are already part of your practice? Which of these strategies do you commit to making part of your practice when designing content for students? Take a moment to set an intention to choose one or two strategies that you will begin implementing tomorrow. Taking steps to implement more of these strategies can have a big impact on how students experience course content on mobile devices.

As educators, creating mobile-friendly course content reduces barriers of access our students may experience when they don't have extended periods of time to dedicate to our course content. By effectively designing course content that leverages moments, we can help to realize the potential of mobile devices for anytime/anywhere learning and create courses that help students realize their dreams ten minutes at a time.

References

Ally, M. (2013). Mobile learning: From research to practice to impact education. *Learning and Teaching in Higher Education: Gulf Perspectives, 10*(2), 3–12.

Andrews, S., Ellis, D.A., Shaw, H., & Piwek, L. (2015). Beyond self-report: Tools to compare estimated and real-world smartphone use. *PloS One, 10*(10), 1–9. 10.1371/journal.pone.0139004

Aslanian, C.B., & Clinefelter, D.L. (2012). *Online college students 2012: Comprehensive data on demands and preferences.* The Learning House, Inc.

Baldwin, S.J., & Ching, Y.H. (2020). Guidelines for designing online courses for mobile devices. *TechTrends*, *64*(3), 413–422.

Barden, O., & Bygroves, M. (2018). 'I wouldn't be able to graduate if it wasn't for my mobile phone.' The affordances of mobile devices in the construction of complex academic texts. *Innovations in Education and Teaching International*, *55*(5), 555–565. 10.1080/14703297.2017.1322996

Farley, H., Murphy, A., Johnson, C., Carter, B., Lane, M., Midgley, W., Hafeez-Baig, A., Dekeyser, S., & Koronios, A. (2015). How do students use their mobile devices to support learning? A case study from an Australian regional university. *Journal of Interactive Media in Education*, *2015*(1), 1–13. 10.5334/jime.ar

López, F.A. & Silva, M.M. (2014). M-learning patterns in the virtual classroom. *Mobile Learning Applications in Higher Education*, *11*(1), 208–221.

Moore, C. (2020). Now is the time to embrace mobile learning. *EDUCAUSE Review*. https://er.educause.edu/blogs/2020/6/now-is-the-time-to-embrace-mobile-learning

Murray, M.C., Pérez, J., Geist, D., & Hedrick, A. (2012). Student interaction with online course content: Build it and they might come. *Journal of Information Technology Education: Research*, *11*(1), 125–140.

National Center for Education Statistics. (2021, October). *School Survey on Crime and Safety*. https://nces.ed.gov/programs/digest/d21/tables/dt21_233.50.asp

Seilhamer, R., Chen, B., Bauer, S., Salter, A., & Bennett, L. (2018). Changing mobile learning practices: A multiyear study 2012–2016. *EDUCAUSE Review*. https://er.educause.edu/articles/2018/4/changing-mobile-learning-practices-a-multiyear-study-2012–2016

Zimmerman, T.D. (2012). Exploring learner to content interaction as a success factor in online courses. *International Review of Research in Open and Distributed Learning*, *13*(4), 152–165. 10.19173/irrodl.v13i4.1302

PART 3

HOW DO I DESIGN ASSIGNMENTS STUDENTS CAN COMPLETE ON THEIR PHONES?

6

ALLOW CHOICE

CREATING OPPORTUNITIES FOR STUDENTS TO MOVE BETWEEN DEVICES

Empowering students through choice

Integrating opportunities for choice in a course creates an empowering learning experience for students. When I began teaching high school, one of the first strategies I learned was to offer students choice. Sometimes this meant that students would choose the topic or modality of their essay. Other times this meant I would ask students if they would like to write their essay with a blue pen or a red pen. Whether I was offering choice on something seemingly inconsequential (e.g., the color of a pen) or seemingly more important (e.g., the topic of an assignment), creating opportunities for choice changed the classroom climate. Students became empowered as it became clear that our classroom was learner-centered.

Incorporating student choice in assessment can support engagement (Arendt et al., 2016; Pinchot & Paullet, 2021), satisfaction (Arendt et al., 2016; Lin & Overbaugh, 2007), and student learning (Arendt et al., 2016; Pinchot & Paullet, 2021). As educators, we strive to provide individual

DOI: 10.4324/9781003328773-9

learning experiences to students. Assessments that integrate student choice help to create a learner-centered experience in which students have the opportunity to tailor the course to their interests and passions.

Mobile design principle #4: Allow choice

Creating assignments that allow students to choose which device they will use to create and submit provides students the opportunity to move fluidly between their phone and computer depending on what works best for them in that moment. Mobile devices remove limitations on space and time and "amplify the learner's ability to determine and direct their learning by choosing or creating an appropriate context for their learning" (Narayan et al., 2019). Educators can create the opportunity to support student choice and ownership of learning by providing students a choice on whether they submit an assignment on a computer or on their phone, or some combination of the two.

Although some students in our courses may rely solely on their mobile devices to complete assignments, we are also serving students who move fluidly between mobile devices and computers to complete their coursework. As a consumer, we may notice this same pattern in our own behavior. For example, each week I order produce online. Depending on where I am, I may order produce while waiting to pick my daughter up from school. Other times, I may order produce on my laptop when taking a mental break from writing. Sometimes, I'll order everything I need on my laptop and then remember I need blueberries while walking into work. In this case, I'll use my phone to quickly add blueberries to my cart. In each of these cases, I appreciate being able to order my groceries on the device that is most convenient for me. I'm also willing to guess that if I couldn't move fluidly between a laptop and a phone and so easily integrate ordering groceries into my day, I likely would forget to add that last item (e.g., blueberries) if I had to wait to log in to my account on a computer.

Moving fluidly between my laptop and phone allows me to order groceries more easily. Along the same lines, assignments that facilitate seamless movements between a computer and a phone help to allow students to interact more consistently with assignments throughout the day. Assignments in which students can move fluidly between computers and mobile devices create opportunities for "serendipitous learning" (Narayan, 2019, p. 96). Moving fluidly between devices helps to support serendipitous learning as students can incorporate inspiration and thoughts into an assignment as they arise on their phone, just as I can add blueberries to my cart while walking to work.

In addition, strategically leveraging a combination of mobile devices and computers can help to maximize the benefits of each. For example, an EDUCAUSE Quick Poll of over 1,500 students found learners used a combination of laptops and smartphones to make progress in their courses (Robert, 2021). Although some students noted the benefit of using a smartphone for learning in case their laptop stopped working, other students noted that there were specific affordances their phone offered for assignments. For example, one student noted their phone took better pictures than their computer. Students also noted the benefit of using a laptop and a phone at the same time so they could more effectively multitask (Robert, 2021). By creating assignments in which students can choose to use a computer or a mobile device, we can create a flexible learning experience for students to make the best use of the tools to which they have access.

The following sections will provide strategies to design assignments that encourage students to choose which device they will use and encourage instructors to focus on grading for the content, not the device. The beauty of these strategies is that it doesn't require instructors to redesign assignments (Al-Okaily, 2013). These strategies can be applied to existing assignments with little time investment on the part of the instructor. These strategies also help to support fluid movement between devices. Although some students could choose to work exclusively on a computer or a phone, these strategies allow students to leverage the unique benefits of mobile devices and computers to create high-quality assignments.

Providing choice in device type

Perhaps the easiest strategy to design mobile-friendly assignments is to simply add an assignment option that allows students to use their mobile device. Providing students mobile-friendly options can be an easy way to start designing mobile-friendly assignments while being mindful of our time as instructors. By letting students choose how they want to submit, we can create opportunities for students to leverage their mobile device to complete an assignment and to move between devices depending on their needs.

In my work with faculty, I have found that this strategy works especially well for math or chemistry instructors. For example, let's imagine that students have ten practice problems they need to work through for their homework. One way students could submit their assignment would be to download a Word document, write their responses using equation editors, save, and then submit. However, as educators we can make this assignment easily mobile-friendly with two simple steps. First, we could add the questions directly to the LMS so students wouldn't need to download a Word document. Then, we can provide students the option to write their responses on a blank sheet of paper and use their phone to take a picture or scan with a free document scanning app and submit their handwritten responses. A benefit of this approach is that students can choose which way they prefer to submit their responses. Some students may prefer to write their responses instead of struggling with typing equations in an equation editor. Other students may find that the tactile experience of writing their responses on a sheet of paper helps them to better retain and understand the material.

This strategy is a quick and easy way to leverage student choice to create mobile-friendly assignments. Not only can this strategy provide students the opportunity to complete an assignment in a way that best aligns with their preferences and needs, but it can also overcome the limitation of small screens (Eschenbrenner & Nah, 2019). As students can complete their assignment by writing responses on a sheet of paper, it expands the screen size even beyond some computer screens. It effectively creates the experience of using dual monitors. Students can use their phone to see the questions while they write their responses on a sheet of 8 ½ x 11 paper. By choosing what they will submit, students can overcome the limitation of small screens if they use a mobile device.

This strategy also helps to support students in moving fluidly between devices. They may begin the assignment by viewing the practice problems on a computer while they write their answers on a sheet of paper. Then, they can use their phone to scan and submit their assignment. In this example, students can leverage the devices they have access to at that moment to work through the practice problems more easily and fluidly.

We can also empower students to choose which device they will use by writing directions that work for any medium (Al-Okaily, 2013). Students may have access to and use many different devices, so it is important to include directions that work across devices (Baldwin & Ching, 2020). Although this may seem daunting at first, there are some simple strategies we can use that will help us create directions that work whether a student is using a phone or a computer or moving between these two devices.

First, we can be sure to use device-agnostic language in our assignment directions. Students using a touch screen will not click, but rather tap. As discussed in Chapter 4, we can create device-neutral directions (and communicate acceptance of mobile-device usage) by simply guiding students to "click or tap."

Second, we can provide help documentation to guide students on how to complete an assignment on their mobile device and computer. By including step-by-step documentation for iOS, Android, Windows, and Mac users, we can help support students as they leverage the tools they have to complete assignments. LMSs will often have step-by-step instructions (and sometimes videos) for iOS, Android, Windows, and Mac users. In addition, when we use external tools (e.g., Flip, Padlet, Jamboard), we can often find step-by-step directions for different devices and operating systems that are maintained and created by that company. Providing students links to directions maintained by the tool or LMS can be a win-win for students and instructors. For students, the directions are often detailed and include images for each step. For instructors, we can rest assured that as the tool goes through development phases, any changes in the directions will be updated by the company (Box 6.1).

BOX 6.1 REFLECTION

Let's take a moment to reflect. Are there assignments in your course in which you could simply add an option for students to submit a picture or scanned version of a handwritten assignment? Are there assignments in which you could include directions for submissions for iOS, Android, Mac, and Windows devices?

Grading for content, not device

As instructors, we can also support student choice by ensuring that student grades reflect the content of their assignments and not the device they used to complete the assignment. Grounding assignments in the learning outcome allows students to choose which tool they want to use to complete an assignment and move between a computer and a mobile device as appropriate. As instructors, focusing on the learning outcomes also helps us to ensure that assignments are designed to measure the learning and not the technology.

The first step is to focus on learning outcomes not on the device (Al-Okaily, 2013). As we review our expectations for assignments, it is important to remove expectations as they relate to specific technologies. Let's imagine that one of the learning outcomes in a biology course is "Students will be able to explain mitosis." This learning outcome does not dictate which device students should use to complete the assignment or even how they will explain mitosis. In this case, I can be sure to create an assessment that does not add additional requirements that are not reflected in the learning outcome. For example, I could create an assignment in which students explain mitosis in a:

- 2- to 5-minute video,
- drawing,
- slides presentation, or a
- 200-word essay.

By offering these options, students can choose to use their phone to record a short video in which they explain mitosis. Students could create a drawing that effectively explains the processes involved in mitosis and then use their phone to upload a scanned image of the drawing. Both options could easily be completed on a mobile device. Students could also choose to create a slide presentation using PowerPoint, Google Slides, or Adobe Express. Depending on which tool they choose to use, they might find it more convenient to complete on their computer or their phone. Students could also type a short essay. This approach would likely be most convenient on a computer. Students could also choose to take pictures with their phone that they could use in their presentation explaining mitosis and then add those pictures to their presentation on their computer.

By allowing students these choices, not only is the assignment mobile-friendly, but students also have the opportunity to demonstrate their learning in a modality of their choosing. Students can also choose to move fluidly between devices to incorporate their lived experiences as examples in the explanation of mitosis. Learning outcomes typically focus on what students should learn, not the device they should use to demonstrate their learning. As an instructor, all I need to do is ensure the assignment that I create to assess the learning outcome does not add additional restrictions that are not present in the outcome itself.

Once we have created an assignment that focuses on the outcomes not the device, we need to ensure success criteria apply across mediums (Al-Okaily, 2013). In the assignment in which students explain mitosis, students can choose to create a video, a drawing, a presentation, or an essay. These options are agnostic of a specific technology. Students can choose to use a camera on their phone, video recording tools in a LMS, Google Slides, PowerPoint, Prezi, Adobe Express, Word documents, Google docs, and many other tools. In developing the success criteria for this assignment, I'll be sure to not name a specific technology as this can limit students' options to use mobile devices. For example, instead of creating a rubric in which I evaluate student use of PowerPoint slides to explain mitosis, I can create a rubric that breaks down the specific aspects of mitosis students need to be sure to explain. Students would likely struggle to create a PowerPoint on their phone. However, they could easily create a slide presentation using Adobe Express on their phone. Students could also strategically use their phone to record short videos that they later add to a presentation when they are at a computer. Ensuring that success criteria work across mediums creates opportunities for students to choose the tool and the device that works best for them to complete an assignment. Focusing success criteria on the learning outcome, not the device or tool, also helps us as educators ensure that we are grounding our grading on the learning outcomes (Box 6.2).

BOX 6.2 REFLECTION

Let's take a moment to reflect. Are there assignments in your course in which you could create choices for students to demonstrate achievement of learning outcomes? What success criteria could align with the learning outcome?

Leveraging the tools students have in their pockets

Student choice provides an opportunity for instructors to create mobile-friendly assignments while also supporting learning and empowering students. In this chapter, we explored the following strategies to create mobile-friendly assessments through choice (Box 6.3).

BOX 6.3 MOBILE DESIGN IN ACTION

ALLOW CHOICE

- Providing Choice in Device Type
    - Let students take a picture of assignments and upload
    - Write directions that work for any medium
- Grading Content, Not Device
    - Focus on the outcomes not on the device
    - Ensure success criteria apply across mediums

The strategies discussed in this chapter range from small changes we can make as instructors to larger assignment redesigns. Choice is a central component of leveraging the tools students already have in their pocket to support student learning. Student choice also provides an opportunity to minimize the limitations of mobile devices for learning. By providing students the option to write their answers on a sheet of paper and submit a scanned version of the assignment with their phone, we can overcome the limitation of a small screen.

Choice is a helpful approach to mobile-friendly assessments as not all students will choose to complete assignments on their phone. Students

BOX 6.4 REFLECTION

Now let's take a moment to reflect on these strategies. Which of these strategies are already part of your practice? Which of these strategies do you commit to making part of your practice when creating assignments for students? Take a moment to set an intention to choose one or two strategies that you will begin implementing tomorrow. Taking steps to implement more of these strategies can have a big impact on how students can leverage mobile devices to submit and create assignments.

may also decide to complete assignments on their phone one week and a computer the next. They may also choose to move fluidly between devices throughout a day and depending on the task. By creating assignments with choice, students can move fluidly between devices depending on their needs and their lives that day (Box 6.4).

References

Al-Okaily, R. (2013). Device neutral assignments for mobile learning in an English language classroom. *QScience Proceedings*, *2013*(3), 29.

Arendt, A., Trego, A., & Allred, J. (2016). Students reach beyond expectations with cafeteria style grading. *Journal of Applied Research in Higher Education*, *8*(1), 2–17. 10.1108/JARHE-03-2014-0048

Baldwin, S.J., & Ching, Y.H. (2020). Guidelines for designing online courses for mobile devices. *TechTrends*, *64*(3), 413–422.

Eschenbrenner, B., & Nah, F.F.H. (2019). Learning through mobile devices: Leveraging affordances as facilitators of engagement. *International Journal of Mobile Learning and Organisation*, *13*(2), 152–170. 10.1504/ijmlo.2019.098193

Lin, S.Y., & Overbaugh, R.C. (2007). The effect of student choice of online discussion format on tiered achievement and student satisfaction. *Journal of Research on technology in Education*, *39*(4), 399–415.

Narayan, V., Herrington, J., & Cochrane, T. (2019). Design principles for heutagogical learning: Implementing student-determined learning with mobile and social media tools. *Australasian Journal of Educational Technology*, *35*(3). 86–101. 10.14742/ajet.3941

Pinchot, J., & Paullet, K. (2021). Using student choice in assignments to create a learner-centered environment for online courses. *Information Systems Education Journal*, *19*(2), 15–24.

Robert, J. (2021). EDUCAUSE QuickPoll results: Flexibility and equity for student success. *EDUCAUSE Review*. https://er.educause.edu/articles/2021/11/educause-quickpoll-results-flexibility-and-equity-for-student-success

7

INTEGRATE MULTIMODALITY

MAKING USE OF ROBUST FEATURES

Making use of robust features

When I started my teaching credential, my parents, my husband, and I got our first iPhones. It was 2010, and they were free at AT&T, because they were the first generation of iPhones. The first thing my mom and I did was take a picture together. Even though the image was grainy, we were both amazed that the image was so clear when compared to images we had taken with our old flip phones. Since 2010, mobile devices have become increasingly sophisticated with robust features that help anyone record high-quality videos, take professional pictures, and record clear audio. The robust features in mobile devices mean that students have access to powerful tools to create assignments that integrate modalities like audio, video, and images.

DOI: 10.4324/9781003328773-10

Mobile design principle #5: Integrate multimodality

Multimodal assignments are inherently mobile-friendly as they mitigate the limitations of mobile devices while maximizing the benefits. As discussed in Chapter 2, some benefits of mobile devices include:

- anytime/anywhere learning (Ally, 2013; Barden & Bygroves, 2018),
- portability (Attenborough & Abbott, 2018; Kobus et al., 2013),
- convenience (Barden & Bygroves, 2018), and
- connection (Cochrane & Bateman, 2010; Cross, 2019; Danish & Hmelo-Silver, 2020; Nasser, 2014).

A video-based discussion on a platform like Flip provides an example of how a multimodal assignment can maximize the benefits of mobile devices for learning. In terms of anytime/anywhere learning and portability, students could use their mobile device to record a short video for that week's Flip discussion while they are with their kids at the park. In this case, the multimodal assignment allows students to complete their assignment anytime/anywhere with a portable device, but it also helps to make the assignment more convenient as students can take advantage of the in-between moments of the day for learning. In addition, this multimodal assignment can help students build a deeper sense of interaction and connection with other students. Perhaps other students in the class watch the video and share that they too are also parents.

Multimodal assignments can also help to minimize the limitations of mobile devices. These limitations include:

- attention pulling (Barden & Bygroves, 2018),
- small screens (Eschenbrenner & Nah, 2019), and
- negative perceptions of mobile device usage for learning (Ally, 2013; Barden & Bygroves, 2018).

For example, let's imagine an assignment in which students are asked to teach the concept of mitosis to their peers. Let's also imagine that the instructor gives students the choice to teach the concept by creating a video, recording a podcast, designing an infographic, or writing a one-pager. In this example, the instructor may link to or provide some tutorials on how to submit a video, audio file, or image to an LMS using an Android or iPhone. Before the assignment is due, the instructor could send a quick reminder to students that the due date is quickly approaching, along with a link to the assignment. A student could receive this reminder while they are scrolling through TikTok and tap the link to open the assignment. Since the assignment can be created on a mobile device, they could begin working on the assignment. In this case, their attention was pulled from TikTok to their assignment. The assignment also helps to mitigate the limitation of small screens as students don't have to try to write their one-pager on a small screen. Instead, they can complete activities that are well-suited to the screen of a phone like recording a video or audio. Finally, because the instructor includes directions for mobile devices, it can help students feel that they have permission to use their phone for learning.

The following sections explore how to scaffold multimodal assignments and how to leverage multimodal assignments to create opportunities for meaningful interactions. The strategies discussed in these sections allow educators to effectively leverage multimodal assignments and create a mobile-friendly experience for students that maximizes the benefits of mobile devices while minimizing the limitations.

Building toward multimodal assignments

Multimodal assignments can be intimidating for both instructors and students. As instructors, we may worry that we may not be able to offer students technical support when creating multimodal assignments. Students may be accustomed to text-centric assignments and nervous about creating assignments that leverage audio, video, and images. When integrating multimodal assignments, both students and instructors benefit from starting small.

Before we can effectively scaffold multimodal assignments, we need to first develop an understanding of the tools to which students have access (Blair, 2015). Although smartphone ownership is nearly ubiquitous in 18- to 29-year-olds (Pew Research Center, 2021), students may have variable access to:

- unlimited data,
- the newest phone, and/or
- storage space.

As instructors, understanding the tools to which our students have access will allow us to support students more effectively as they create multimodal assignments. To gain an understanding of the tools students have, we can simply add a few questions to a survey at the beginning of the semester. Surveying students at the beginning of the semester helps us to build awareness of our students and is a foundational strategy for humanizing education (Pacansky-Brock et al., 2020). In addition to questions about student preference for written or audio feedback, we can also ask students what tools they have and how they use technology in their daily lives. Box 7.1 provides some sample survey questions.

BOX 7.1 UNDERSTANDING STUDENT TECHNOLOGY ACCESS

1. I have [check all that apply]:
   a. A smartphone
   b. A tablet
   c. A laptop
   d. A desktop computer
2. Some challenges that I face when using my laptop or computer are [check all that apply]:
   a. It takes a while to turn on.
   b. I don't have reliable internet at home.
   c. I share it with members of my household.
   d. None! My computer/laptop works great:)
3. Some challenges that I face when using my phone are [check all that apply]:
   a. It takes a while for things to load.
   b. My phone is more than five years old, so not all apps work.
   c. I don't have a lot of storage space for apps on my phone.
   d. I share it with members of my household.
   e. I have limited data.
   f. None. My phone works great!
4. I have access to [check all that apply]:
   a. Microsoft Word, PowerPoint, and Excel
   b. Google docs, Google slides, and Google sheets
   c. Adobe Pro
   d. Other ...

5. I am comfortable using [check all that apply]:
    a. Microsoft Word, PowerPoint, and Excel
    b. Google docs, Google slides, and Google sheets
    c. Adobe Pro
    d. Adobe Express
    e. Canvas Studio
    f. Flip
    g. Discord
    h. My phone to record videos and take pictures
    i. Other ...
6. Is there anything else you would like to share about your access to technology?
7. Is there anything else you would like to share about which technologies you use in your day-to-day life?

These sample questions can also be adapted to specific teaching contexts and student populations. For example, if you know that there are some areas of town that don't have access to reliable internet, it may be helpful to include a question on this topic. In addition, you may want to remove or add specific tools to question 5 depending on specific assignments in your course.

After we have developed an understanding of which tools students have and any challenges they may face, we can prompt students to reflect on the multimodal skills they already have developed (Blair, 2015). Many students are already interacting daily with multimodal content, whether it be via TikTok, Instagram, or podcasts. Students may also be creating multimodal posts for Instagram that strategically combine text and images/video to convey a message. Although students interact with multimodal content every day, they may not see how the skills in creating an Instagram post would translate into the classroom.

As such, one way we can build towards multimodal assignments is to prompt students to reflect on how they create multimodal content in their daily lives (Blair, 2015). The reflection could be something as simple as a video discussion at the beginning of the semester and could serve the dual purpose of acting as an icebreaker. This reflection can help students to identify skills they are already developing in their personal lives and how these skills apply to their academic lives.

Once students have reflected on how they already use multimodal tools in their daily lives, they can create tech tutorials for their peers on how to use a particular tool. As instructors, it can be difficult to provide students support and guidance on how to use the plethora of technologies that they can use to create multimodal assignments. Supporting students as they work to use technologies on a variety of devices and platforms can feel like a Sisyphean task. However, when students create tech tutorials for their peers, we can alleviate some of the pressure on us while empowering students to share their expertise on technology.

Blair (2015) noted that these tech tutorials, or "digital demos," help to empower students and encourage students to "view themselves as co-equal participants in the course and collaborative knowledge-makers" (p. 480). Students can use a variety of modalities to create these guides. By providing students the chance to create an infographic, short video, or written guide, we can also encourage students to explore and play with different modalities and tools while leveraging their phone if they so choose. We can also collect these tech tutorials with the permission of our students to share in future courses.

The next step in building toward multimodal assignments is to prompt students to move from "consumption to production" (Blair, 2015, p. 479). Although we may assume that students today are expert technology users and can easily create multimodal assignments, the truth is the myth of the digital native is nothing more than a myth (Kirschner & De Bruyckere, 2017). Students today may use their phones frequently throughout their day for personal use, but many students need guidance on how to use their phones for learning and professional purposes (Kirschner & De Bruyckere, 2017). Although students may consume multimodal content in their personal lives via social media, the internet, podcasts, and streaming services, they produce multimodal content for their courses less frequently (Kennedy & Fox, 2013; Kirschner & De Bruyckere, 2017).

Being able to leverage mobile devices to create multimodal content is an essential skill for 21st-century careers (Harris & Greer, 2021; Narayan, et al., 2019). Many professionals rely on mobile devices in their careers (Harris & Greer, 2021; Narayan, et al., 2019). As such, leveraging mobile devices for the creation and production of multimodal assessments helps students to experiment with skills they will need to be successful in their future careers.

We can support students in moving from "consumption to production" (Blair, 2015, p. 479) by designing authentic multimodal assessments that prepare students for future careers (Blair, 2015; Harris & Greer, 2021). When we design authentic assessments, we need to ensure that the assessments reflect the real world, require innovation, pull together many skills, and integrate opportunities for feedback (Wiggins & McTighe, 2005). We can create multimodal authentic assessments by providing opportunities for students to use their mobile devices to produce content in ways that mirror the real world and their future careers. These assessments will vary based on discipline, but one could imagine ways in which a business instructor could create an assignment in which students do the following:

- choose a business they will create,
- design a social media marketing strategy, and
- create a website that generates a multichannel experience for consumers.

By creating multimodal assessments, students can not only leverage mobile devices in the assignment, but they can also explore ways in which their mobile devices will help them succeed in their professional lives. In this way, we are offering students important guidance and support in learning how to use the incredible technology they carry in their pockets.

Multimodal assignments are inherently mobile-friendly as they leverage the unique robust features of smartphones for learning. However, multimodal assignments can be intimidating for both students and instructors. As such, starting small and gaining a sense of the technologies students have access to and how they are accustomed to using those technologies can provide a helpful starting point. Once this foundation is laid, instructors can encourage students to create guides for peers on technologies with which they are already familiar. Then, instructors can help students work to take what they know from consuming multimodal content and begin to create their own multimodal content. Finally, as students become more comfortable, instructors can create opportunities for students to leverage their mobile devices to create sophisticated multimodal assignments just as they would in their future careers.

Supporting interaction with multimodal assignments

Multimodal assignments can also provide opportunities for meaningful, mobile-friendly interactions in a course. Meaningful interactions within a course support student learning (Cung et al., 2018; Sher, 2009), satisfaction (Sher, 2009), and retention (Mitchell & Hughes, 2014). Within a course, there are many different types of interactions that a student can experience, including:

- interactions with other students (Moore, 1989),
- interactions with the instructor (Moore, 1989), and
- interactions with the content (Moore, 1989).

Student interactions with other students could include discussions, group projects, think-pair-shares, and other collaborative activities. Students can interact with instructors during office hours and through emails, feedback, and discussions. Interactions with content can occur when students are accessing course content or completing assignments. In this section, we'll explore ways in which we can use mobile devices to support student–student and student–instructor interactions through multimodal assignments.

Multimodal assignments help to support interaction whether we are teaching face-to-face, online, or some combination of the two. Although interactions can occur in face-to-face classes, incorporating opportunities for multimodal interactions can allow student learning and interaction to transcend the walls of a classroom and the limited amount of time we have face-to-face with our students. In online courses, multimodal interactions are especially important as a reliance on text-based interactions in online courses can create situations where miscommunication between faculty and students occurs (Grigoryan, 2017). In addition, multimodal interactions in online courses provide an opportunity to build relationships as our interactions become humanized (Pacansky-Brock et al., 2020).

Supporting student–student interactions through multimodal assignments

Multimodal assignments provide an opportunity to support meaningful student–student interactions while also taking steps toward creating mobile-friendly courses. Although discussion boards are frequently used to support interaction, these can be difficult for students to contribute to on a phone. When a student accesses a text-based discussion board on a phone, they will experience a seemingly endless scroll trying to see all the discussion posts. However, video- and audio-based discussion platforms make it much easier for students to contribute to the discussion and review peers' contributions on their phone. In addition to being mobile-friendly, the video-based discussion provides an opportunity for student–student interactions to "be on a more personal level" (Swartzwelder et al., 2019, p. 6). Video discussions can allow students to build meaningful interactions with each other and to get to know their classmates in a more profound way.

Multimodal assignments can also create mobile-friendly courses while supporting group work. Multimodal collaborative assignments create opportunities for students to work together to create infographics, presentations, videos, or podcasts (Harris & Greer, 2021). Although group assignments are notoriously difficult to design so everyone in the group contributes in meaningful ways, multimodal assignments provide an opportunity for students to let passion drive their contributions to the assignment. Perhaps one student enjoys writing (I know, but there are some of us out there) while another student enjoys taking photos. Together they could create a powerful infographic or social media post that pulls together the written word and images taken with a phone.

Supporting student–instructor interactions through multimodal assignments

As instructors, we can help lay the foundation for meaningful interactions with our students by leveraging audio and video to provide overviews of assignments and to provide feedback. By making use of audio and video to introduce assignments and provide feedback, we can model effective methods for multimodal production that can inspire students in their own multimodal assignments.

As instructors, one of the most powerful ways we can support students in creating multimodal assignments is to model the creation of videos. Creating a short video overview of an upcoming assignment can be a great way to model to students how we can leverage multimodal content (and our phones) for learning. Creating imperfect videos can also help students feel connected to us as instructors (Pacansky-Brock et al., 2020). When I was teaching faculty during the pandemic on how to build classroom communities online, I created short overview videos for upcoming assignments. My daughter was four at the time and always singing in the background (she's always been able to project). Instead of rerecording or trying to keep my house perfectly quiet, I would just say, "And that's my daughter again singing in the background. It's almost bath time." Four years later, faculty who were in the course still ask how my daughter is and share that this was one of their favorite parts of the course. It brought some levity to a difficult time.

Assignment overview videos may not provide us the same sense of interaction with students that we experience in face-to-face interactions, but they do offer an important opportunity for students to get to know us. These videos help to lay the foundation for meaningful interactions and relationships with students in our courses. To build relationships, we need to know who our students are, and they in turn need to know who we are. These short videos provide an opportunity for students to get to know us and who we are. When we embed these videos directly into our LMS, students are able to view these assignment overview videos easily on their phone. They can simply tap the play button while riding the bus to work or school, waiting in line at the grocery store, or brushing their teeth. We may even choose to create these assignment overview videos on our phones. Using our phones to create these videos can help show students the power of the technology to which they already have access and destigmatize the use of mobile devices for learning.

Another way we can leverage multimodal tools to create mobile-friendly assignments is by providing students audio/video feedback. Feedback provides a powerful opportunity for interaction (Rockey, 2019) and can provide an opportunity to build meaningful relationships with our students. However, mismanaged feedback can create seemingly insurmountable rifts between us and our students. Providing feedback is an art. As instructors, we want to be sure to provide feedback that supports students, lifts them up, but also helps push them to achieve greatness.

Constructive feedback helps students to recognize their strengths and actionable ways they can grow. One barrier in providing constructive feedback to students can be a reliance on text-based feedback. Misunderstandings are more common when we are communicating via writing. I'm sure many of us have noted in our personal lives that miscommunications can arise when we are texting or sending emails. As educators, when we rely on text-based feedback it is more likely that students will misunderstand our tone and interpret our feedback as harsher than we intended (Grigoryan, 2017).

Providing audio/video feedback can help to mitigate misunderstandings as we are able to use our voice to communicate the tone of our constructive feedback in more nuanced ways (Grigoryan, 2017). In addition, audio/video feedback is easier for students to access on a mobile device. Instead of having to try to work through the text-based feedback on a small screen, students can simply tap play and hear our voice. To ensure that we meet accessibility standards, we can ask students at the beginning of the semester in a survey if they prefer audio or written feedback. This can help us ensure that if students prefer written feedback, we can make a note of that and provide feedback to students in the way that works best for them.

For students to learn and thrive in our courses, we need to create meaningful opportunities for students to interact with each other and with ourselves as their instructor. Multimodal assignments provide opportunities for students to interact with each other through video-based discussions and to collaborate on the creation of assignments while leveraging their mobile devices for learning. As instructors, we can lay the foundation for meaningful interactions with our students by modeling multimodal content through assignment overview videos. We can also provide audio/video feedback that limits miscommunications common in text-based communication (Grigoryan, 2017). Multimodal assignments provide unique opportunities for students to interact with each other and their instructors while using their phones for learning.

Scaffolding multimodal assignments and leveraging multimodal assignments for interaction

Multimodal assignments are inherently mobile-friendly as they leverage the robust features students already have access to in their mobile devices. In addition, multimodal assignments help to maximize the benefits of phones for learning while minimizing the limitations. However, it is important to remember that while students may consume multimodal content throughout their day, they have less experience in creating their own multimodal content (Kennedy & Fox, 2013; Kirschner & De Bruyckere, 2017). As such, to effectively integrate multimodal assignments we need to strategically build towards more complicated production of multimodal content while mindfully integrating opportunities for multimodal interactions. In this chapter, we explored the following strategies to create multimodal assignments that make use of mobile devices for learning (Box 7.2):

BOX 7.2 MOBILE DESIGN IN ACTION

INTEGRATE MULTIMODALITY

- Building Towards Multimodal Assignments
    - Understand what tools students have
    - Prompt students to reflect on multimodal skills
    - Empower students to create tech tutorials for peers
    - Help students become producers
- Supporting Interaction with Multimodal Assignments
    - Leverage video for robust discussions
    - Design collaborative multimodal assignments
    - Embed assignment overview videos
    - Provide audio/video feedback

Mobile devices provide important tools for 21st-century careers and relationships. By building towards multimodal assignments, we can help students develop skills they will need to be successful in their future careers. Professionals rely more and more on their phones to create multimodal content in their working careers. Whether they are creating short videos for engaging presentations or managing a social media campaign, professionals need to be able to compose high-quality content on their mobile devices. Integrating multimodal assignments in our courses helps students to not only use their mobile device for learning, but also develop essential skills to leverage this tool in their future careers. Multimodal assignments also provide an important opportunity for students to interact with each other and us as instructors. Leveraging the multimodal features of mobile devices can help us to create meaningful interactions that help to not only build community, but also alleviate miscommunications that can arise when we rely on text-based communication. When we integrate multimodal assignments in our classes, we can help students to use their mobile devices to practice the skills they will increasingly need for successful careers and relationships in the 21st century (Box 7.3).

BOX 7.3 REFLECTION

Now let's take a moment to reflect on these strategies. Which of these strategies are already part of your practice? Which of these strategies do you commit to making part of your practice when creating assignments for students? Take a moment to set an intention to choose one or two strategies that you will begin implementing tomorrow. Taking steps to implement more of these strategies can have a big impact on how students can leverage mobile devices to submit and create assignments.

References

Ally, M. (2013). Mobile learning: From research to practice to impact education. *Learning and Teaching in Higher Education: Gulf Perspectives, 10*(2), 3–12.

Attenborough, J.A., & Abbott, S. (2018). Leave them to their own devices: Healthcare students' experiences of using a range of mobile devices for learning. *International Journal for the Scholarship of Teaching and Learning, 12*(2), 16.

Barden, O., & Bygroves, M. (2018). 'I wouldn't be able to graduate if it wasn't for my mobile phone.' The affordances of mobile devices in the construction of complex academic texts. *Innovations in Education and Teaching International, 55*(5), 555–565. 10.1080/14703297.2017.1322996

Blair, K.L. (2015). Teaching multimodal assignments in OWI contexts. In B. Hewett & K.E. DePew. (Eds.), *Foundational practices of online writing instruction*. WAC Clearinghouse.

Cochrane, T., & Bateman, R. (2010). Smartphones give you wings: Pedagogical affordances of mobile Web 2.0. *Australasian Journal of Educational Technology*, *26*(1). 10.14742/ajet.1098

Cross, S. (2019). How handheld devices transform, augment and reinforce university students' study habits: emerging themes from a three-year study. *EDULEARN19 Proceedings*, 6028–6034.

Cung, B., Xu, D., & Eichhorn, S. (2018). Increasing interpersonal interactions in an online course: Does increased instructor email activity and voluntary meeting time in a physical classroom facilitate student learning? *Online Learning*, *22*(3), 193–215.

Danish, J., & Hmelo-Silver, C.E. (2020). On activities and affordances for mobile learning. *Contemporary Educational Psychology*, *60*, 101829. 10.1016/j.cedpsych.2019.101829

Eschenbrenner, B., & Nah, F.F.H. (2019). Learning through mobile devices: Leveraging affordances as facilitators of engagement. *International Journal of Mobile Learning and Organisation*, *13*(2), 152–170. 10.1504/ijmlo.2019.098193

Grigoryan, A. (2017). Audiovisual commentary as a way to reduce transactional distance and increase teaching presence in online writing instruction: Student perceptions and preferences. *Journal of Response to Writing*, *3*(1), 83–128.

Harris, H.S., & Greer, M. (2021). Using multimedia for instructor presence in purposeful pedagogy-driven online technical writing courses. *Journal of Technical Writing and Communication*, *51*(1), 31–52. 10.1177/0047281620977162

Kennedy, D.M., & Fox, R. (2013). 'Digital natives': An Asian perspective for using learning technologies. *International Journal of Education and Development using ICT*, *9*(1), 65–79.

Kirschner, P.A., & De Bruyckere, P. (2017). The myths of the digital native and the multitasker. *Teaching and Teacher education*, *67*, 135–142. 10.1016/j.tate.2017.06.001

Kobus, M.B., Rietveld, P., & Van Ommeren, J.N. (2013). Ownership versus on-campus use of mobile IT devices by university students. *Computers & Education*, *68*, 29–41. 10.1016/j.compedu.2013.04.003

Mitchell, Y.F., & Hughes, G.D. (2014). Demographic and instructor-student interaction factors associated with community college students' intent to persist. *Journal of Research in Education*, *24*(2), 63–78.

Moore, M. (1989) Editorial: Three types of interaction. *American Journal of Distance Education*, *3*(2), 1–7. 10.1080/08923648909526659

Narayan, V., Herrington, J., & Cochrane, T. (2019). Design principles for heutagogical learning: Implementing student-determined learning with mobile and social media tools. *Australasian Journal of Educational Technology*, *35*(3). 86-101. 10.14742/ajet.3941

Nasser, R. (2014). Using mobile devices to increase student academic outcomes in Qatar. *Open Journal of Social Sciences*, *2*(02), 67–73. 10.4236/jss.2014.22010

Pacansky-Brock, M., Smedshammer, M., Vincent-Layton, K. (2020). Humanizing online teaching to equitize higher education. *Current Issues in Education*, *21*(2), 1–21.

Pew Research Center (2021). Mobile fact sheet. https://www.pewresearch.org/internet/fact-sheet/mobile/

Rockey, A. (2019). Planning feedback opportunities in online non-writing intensive courses. *Online Literacies Open Resource*. 1–6.

Sher, A. (2009). Assessing the relationship of student-instructor and student-student interaction to student learning and satisfaction in web-based online learning environment. *Journal of Interactive Online Learning*, *8*(2),102–120.

Swartzwelder, K., Murphy, J., & Murphy, G. (2019). The impact of text-based and video discussions on student engagement and interactivity in an online course. *Journal of Educators Online*, *16*(1). 1–7.

Wiggins, G. & McTighe, J. (2005). Understanding by design (2nd ed.). ASCD.

8

LEVERAGE MOBILE-FRIENDLY TOOLS

WORKING SMARTER, NOT HARDER

Working smarter, not harder: Choosing the right tool

Growing up my parents undertook a lot of house projects. When we first moved into our farmhouse in Wisconsin, the upstairs had been used for hay storage and was unlivable. We lived the first few months in the living room of the house while my parents worked at night and on the weekends to make the upstairs inhabitable. Perhaps inspired by their hard work, my husband and I have always bought houses in need of small and large transformations to be livable. As we embarked on our house projects, my dad always advised us to choose the right tool for the job. However, heeding this advice was difficult for my husband and me. We both have a tendency to try to make the wrong tool work so we don't have to buy something new. This has always made our work much harder. Finally, when I saw my husband trying to trim our orange tree with kitchen scissors, my dad's advice sunk in. I bought the right tool, and we were able to easily trim the orange tree (and in half the time).

DOI: 10.4324/9781003328773-11

Mobile design principle #6: Leverage mobile-friendly tools

Choosing the right tool for the job can save us time and make our lives much easier. This lesson applies to mobile design as well. Many companies have already invested quite a bit of time, expertise, and money to design mobile-friendly apps and tools. When we leverage these mobile-friendly tools, we can create mobile-friendly assessments that make the work of creating a mobile-friendly course much easier. When we work smarter and not harder, we can rely on the work that others have already done to create responsive and mobile-friendly experiences.

The following sections explore how we can create mobile-friendly assessments by choosing tools that are already designed to be used on phones.

Making use of the LMS

As instructors, one easy way we can make our courses more mobile-friendly is to move content and assignments directly into our LMS. Many LMSs have associated apps that are designed to make the LMS accessible on mobile devices. By making use of our LMS, we can rely on the expertise of developers who have dedicated time and energy to creating a mobile-friendly experience for the LMS on apps. When a user interface is mobile-friendly, students are more likely to use their mobile device to complete assessments (Nikou & Economides, 2017). Creating user interfaces that are mobile-friendly can seem like a daunting task. Luckily, our LMS has likely already made significant investments in developing an app that creates a positive experience for students using their phones. As instructors, simply making use of our LMS can help us take large strides toward creating mobile-friendly assessments.

The first way we can effectively make use of our LMS for assignments is to familiarize ourselves with the mobile-friendliness of our LMS. To get a sense of the mobile-friendliness of our LMS, we can conduct an internet search to see if our LMS has an app. Once we have determined if our LMS has an app, we can conduct an internet search to better understand recommendations for creating a mobile-friendly experience for students using the LMS. LMSs like Canvas, Blackboard, and Moodle each have unique apps and guidelines for instructors looking to leverage the app to create a mobile-friendly experience for students.

Once we have determined if our LMS has an app and if there are any specific recommendations of which we should be aware, we can move our assignments directly into the LMS. As discussed in Chapter 3, moving content directly into the LMS can help to create mobile-friendly content that also meets accessibility standards. Making use of our LMS also allows us to design mobile-friendly assignments. By moving assignments directly into the LMS, we not only increase the mobile-friendliness of our assignments, but we also make it easier for students to complete the assignment regardless of which device they are using. I found this strategy especially helpful for clarifying assignment directions. For example, when I was teaching an online pedagogy course for faculty, one assignment asked faculty to use an equity rubric to reflect on their courses. The original assignment prompted faculty to download the equity rubric as a Word document, evaluate their course, and then re-upload the equity rubric. To simplify the assignment, I moved each line of the rubric into a quiz in which faculty rated their course on the scale that correlated with the rubric. Faculty then had an open-ended question in which they explained their rating. Moving the rubric into a quiz in my LMS did not take a lot of time, but it did help make it easier for faculty to complete the assignment, regardless of which device they were using.

Finally, we can also make use of our LMS by sending students reminders to complete assignments. Students appreciate receiving reminders about upcoming assignments. Research suggests that reminders delivered on mobile devices help to support student learning (Nasser, 2014) and retention (Boath et al., 2016; Fozdar & Kumar, 2007). In Chapter 5, we discussed the importance of guiding students in setting notifications so they can manage distractions. Reminders also offer an opportunity to redirect student attention back to our assignments. One limitation of using mobile devices for learning is the potential for attention-pulling (Barden & Bygroves, 2018). However, research suggests that reminders can help to pull attention back to the task at hand and minimize unwanted distractions (Draxler et al., 2019).

As instructors, we can make our assignments more mobile-friendly by encouraging students to review their notification settings for the LMS at the beginning of the term. Many LMSs have the option to add a phone number so students can receive reminders via text messages. By leveraging reminders via the LMS, we can help students make progress on assignments in our courses anytime and anywhere. Imagine, for example, a student is riding the bus to work and gets a reminder on their phone that a discussion post is due that evening. The reminder includes a link to the assignment. As it's a video-based discussion, the student decides to complete it once they are off the bus. The student spends the rest of the bus ride planning out what to talk about in their discussion post and reviewing the reading for that week. As the student has young children and is balancing work and school, making use of the in-between moments of their day is crucial for their success.

As educators, making effective use of our LMS for assignments is an easy way to create mobile-friendly assessments. Intentionally leveraging the LMS to create mobile-friendly assignments makes effective use of the expertise that went into building the LMS app. Making use of the LMS app not only helps us to create mobile-friendly assignments with little time investment, but it also helps students complete assignments more easily regardless of the device they are using.

Incorporating mobile-friendly tools to support active learning

Beyond the LMS there are mobile-friendly tools that we can effectively integrate into our courses to support active learning. One of the most profound statements about learning I heard early in my career was "the person who is doing the most talking is doing the most learning." This statement guided my practice as a first-year high school teacher. This phrase would nag at me if I found myself lecturing for more than 15 minutes without providing an opportunity for students to speak. Still, to this day, I often think of this statement when I'm facilitating faculty workshops.

Active learning provides students the opportunity to build their own understanding of a concept through activities that facilitate more complicated thought processes than simply remembering or reiterating (Brame, 2016; Freeman et al., 2014; Prince, 2004). In addition, a crucial component of active learning is prompting students to think about their own learning through metacognition (Bonwell & Eison, 1991; Brame, 2016). The benefits of active learning are tremendous compared to lecture-only courses. Research suggests active learning supports student learning (Freeman et al., 2014; Ruiz-Primo et al., 2011) and student success (Freeman et al., 2014). In addition, research suggests that active learning can help to create inclusive classrooms by closing equity gaps (Haak et al., 2011) and gender gaps (Lorenzo et al., 2006).

Formative assessments are one way instructors can integrate active learning strategies in their classes. In fact, it can be quite difficult to delineate between active learning and formative assessments (Brame, 2016). As Handelsman et al. (2007) noted: "it is hard to imagine an active learning exercise that does not have an assessment component, and assessment is automatically active because the students must **do** something to assess themselves or be assessed" (p. 52). Assessment, particularly formative assessment, is a part of the active learning process in which students construct knowledge and receive feedback on their progress.

Mobile devices can support active learning that extends beyond the walls of a classroom. Formative assessments, when delivered via mobile devices, allow instructors to integrate active learning experiences and increase student learning (Ling et al., 2014). When we integrate mobile-friendly tools to support active learning, we can not only transform our students' experience within the walls of our classrooms, but also effectively create opportunities for students to engage with formative assessments anytime and anywhere. The following sections will explore how we can use polling tools, quizzing apps, virtual spaces, QR codes, and augmented reality (AR) to create meaningful opportunities for active learning through mobile-friendly assessments.

Mobile-friendly polling tools can support active learning by centering the student voice and creating a sense of discovery. Mobile-friendly polling tools like Socrative, Poll Everywhere, Kahoot!, and/or Mentimeter can support active learning both in and out of the classroom (Sun, 2014). Polling tools support student engagement and learning (Sun, 2014). They can even decrease student anxiety (Sun, 2014). In fact, research suggests that when students use their own mobile devices to participate with a polling tool as opposed to a clicker, they will experience a greater decrease in anxiety (Sun, 2014).

One powerful way to integrate polling tools to create mobile-friendly assessments is to create low-stakes quizzes that build community and center the student voice in our courses. For example, an instructor could incorporate student responses from introductory videos into a poll. Then, during class, an instructor could have students contribute to a poll in which they recall the student who shared in their video that they lived in Sweden or watched *Hocus Pocus* 3,000 times. This can be a good way to pull the introductory videos into the classroom, create a sense of community as everyone tries to remember the correct answer, and encourage students to spend some time watching those introductory videos.

Instructors could also use polling tools to have students test a hypothesis. This approach can help students construct their own understanding of a course concept and foster a sense of discovery. For example, if I was teaching statistics, I could ask students to make a prediction about the probability of rolling a six when rolling five dice. Then students could conduct an experiment, and each student could submit their results via a polling tool. As the whole class would be submitting the results of their experiments into the poll repeatedly via their mobile device, the class results would gradually approach the actual probability. Then we could work through the formula that would allow us to confirm the actual probability. In this example, leveraging a mobile-friendly polling tool creates an opportunity to integrate active learning in the classroom through formative assessment and leverage students' mobile devices to help them discover a mathematical concept.

Instructors can also leverage mobile devices to support student self-assessment with quizzing apps. Metacognition and thinking about one's own learning are essential components of active learning (Brame, 2016). Quizzing apps can help to support metacognition and a reflection of learning while students are away from home. Quizzing apps can be used in a variety of ways to support learning. For example, an instructor could create a bank of questions that students respond to throughout the day. Alternatively, as part of an assignment, students could create their own quiz questions. The instructor could review these questions, offer feedback, and create a class bank that everyone could practice with throughout the day. One of the benefits of quizzing apps is that students can study and make use of in-between moments of the day to reflect on their learning. Students will also receive automatic feedback on whether they answered the question correctly or incorrectly. This provides an opportunity for students to reflect on the concepts that they still need to spend time studying.

Mobile-friendly tools can also support active learning in assessments by creating a virtual space for students to receive and provide peer–peer feedback. Students frequently use their mobile devices to socialize with others via social media or texting (Ally & Wark, 2018; Kirschner & De Bruyckere, 2017). By creating a virtual space for students to access and participate with their phone, we can leverage how students already use and like to use their phones. Mobile apps like Discord, Slack, or Nectir can create a virtual space where students check in with their peers for just-in-time feedback.

Perhaps one of the most exciting aspects of these virtual spaces is their ability to disrupt traditional power structures within a classroom. In face-to-face discussions, we may notice that some students always answer our questions. A large body of research works to explore this phenomenon by understanding the power dynamics, identities, and interactions that emerge in the talk of a classroom (e.g., Engle et al., 2014; Philip & Gupta, 2020). Although power and identities can silence some students in classroom discussions (Engle et al., 2014), technologies and virtual spaces can disrupt the power dynamics that can emerge within a classroom to equitize participation (Philip & Gupta, 2020; Sauro, 2009).

Virtual spaces also help to empower students as keepers of knowledge in a classroom and free up instructor time. For example, in a virtual space, students can ask questions to the entire class. Students could upload a picture of an assessment in progress and ask for informal feedback from the group. As instructors, we might find that students will respond even before we have a chance. In this way, the virtual space can create mobile-friendly opportunities for students to connect outside of the classroom, but it also helps to free up some of the instructor's time by democratizing the classroom and empowering students to provide feedback to their peers.

Another way we can leverage mobile-friendly tools is to create our own QR codes. This can be a great opportunity for us to use a mobile-friendly tool that doesn't require students to download another app. Creating a QR code is not difficult and often will only take a minute or less. In fact, in the Chrome browser, I can simply click "Share" and generate a QR code for any website in two clicks. As instructors, we can use QR codes to support active learning both in and out of the classroom. Within the classroom, I could use a QR code to help students access a collaborative document like Padlet and provide an opportunity for a collaborative, formative assessment. I could also create QR codes to support learning outside of the classroom. For example, I could post QR codes around campus to help students on a guided assessment where they can apply their knowledge on the go. I could also create an assignment in which students generate their own QR codes to create a guided nature walk in which students describe particular trees or rock features in an area.

Finally, we can leverage mobile-friendly tools to expand the classroom with AR, which allows users to see their physical surroundings with a digital overlay (Kuo-Hung et al., 2016). Using AR in assessments aligns with active learning principles and can help to make feedback more immediate (Kuo-Hung et al., 2016). AR also can help instructors in designing "transformative pedagogies to empower and engage the learner in the learning process" (Aguayo et al., 2017, p. 35). Although AR for learning is an emerging field, we can consider ways in which we can leverage AR to create assessment experiences for students that take them out into the world. For example, Colin et al. (2021), in a spotlight of mobile learning across University of California campuses, highlighted an instructor's use of Pokémon Go to help students actively construct their own understanding of sampling methods. In this assessment, students were able to leverage their phones to gain a deeper understanding of sampling methods by collecting Pokémon. Just as AR creates a digital overlay on top of our real-world experiences, AR can help students to see how our course creates an overlay over their lived lives. Whether they are at the beach, on campus, or at work, students can pull out their phones and see their course everywhere when we use AR for assessments.

Active learning holds tremendous potential for students to construct knowledge and reflect on their learning. By integrating active learning approaches into our assessments, we can empower students to take charge of their own learning. Mobile-friendly tools provide a unique opportunity to not only integrate active learning, but to also create mobile-friendly assessments. Polling tools can be used in formative assessments to create a sense of discovery and center students' lived experiences in the course. Quizzing apps support metacognition and reflection. Mobile-friendly virtual spaces can disrupt traditional power dynamics in a classroom. QR codes can integrate active learning both in and out of the classroom. AR brings student learning out of the classroom. By leveraging tools that are already mobile-friendly, we can create powerful assessments and active learning experiences for our students that make use of the tools students carry with them always.

Simplifying and transforming assessments with the right tools

When we choose the right tool, we can easily create mobile-friendly assessments for our students. By moving our assessments into an LMS, we can simplify our courses for students (and for ourselves) and make use of the time, expertise, and investments that went into creating a mobile-friendly user experience for students.

Mobile devices are inherently active and can support active learning through formative assessments in ways that create a sense of discovery, foster metacognition, disrupt traditional power dynamics, and expand learning beyond our classrooms. By strategically leveraging the LMS and mobile-friendly tools, we can create assessments that support student learning in expansive and transformative ways. In this chapter, we explored the following strategies to leverage the mobile-friendliness of our LMS and existing tools (Box 8.1):

BOX 8.1 MOBILE DESIGN IN ACTION

LEVERAGE MOBILE-FRIENDLY TOOLS

- Making Use of the LMS
  - Explore the LMS app and mobile-friendly recommendations
  - Move assignments directly into the LMS
  - Send students reminders to complete assignments
- Incorporating Mobile-Friendly Tools to Support Active Learning
  - Use polling tools
  - Support self-assessment with quizzing apps
  - Provide a virtual space for formative peer–peer feedback
  - Create your own QR codes
  - Expand beyond the classroom with AR

By working smarter and not harder, we can help to leverage the affordances of mobile devices to support assessments that students can complete anytime and anywhere via the LMS. We can also help to support active learning through formative assessments that can disrupt traditional power dynamics in the classroom and center the student voice while creating opportunities for metacognition and learning experiences that infuse students' lives 24/7 (Box 8.2).

BOX 8.2 REFLECTION

Now let's take a moment to reflect on these strategies. Which of these strategies are already part of your practice? Which of these strategies do you commit to making part of your practice when creating assignments for students? Take a moment to set an intention to choose one or two strategies that you will begin implementing tomorrow. Taking steps to implement more of these strategies can have a big impact on how students can leverage mobile devices to submit and create assignments.

References

Aguayo, C., Cochrane, T., & Narayan, V. (2017). Key themes in mobile learning: Prospects for learner-generated learning through AR and VR. *Australasian Journal of Educational Technology*, *33*(6). 27–40.

Ally, M., & Wark, N. (2018). Online student use of mobile devices for learning. *World Conference on Mobile and Contextual Learning, 2018*. 8–13.

Barden, O., & Bygroves, M. (2018). 'I wouldn't be able to graduate if it wasn't for my mobile phone.' The affordances of mobile devices in the construction of complex academic texts. *Innovations in Education and Teaching International*, *55*(5), 555–565. 10.1080/14703297.2017.1322996

Boath, E., Jinks, A., Thomas, N., Thompson, R., Evans, J., O'Connell, P., & Taylor, L. (2016). Don't go with the 'FLO': A student mobile texting service to enhance nursing student retention. *Nurse Education Today*, *45*, 80–86. 10.1016/j.nedt.2016.06.019

Bonwell, C.C., & Eison, J.A. (1991). *Active learning: Creating excitement in the classroom. 1991 ASHE-ERIC higher education reports*. ERIC Clearinghouse on Higher Education.

Brame, C. (2016). *Active learning*. Vanderbilt University Center for Teaching. https://cft.vanderbilt.edu/active-learning/

Colin, M., Eastman, S., Merrill, M., & Rockey, A. (2021). Leveraging Mobile Technology to Achieve Teaching Goals. *Educause Review*. https://er.educause.edu/articles/2021/3/leveraging-mobile-technology-to-achieve-teaching-goals

Draxler, F., Schneegass, C., & Niforatos, E. (2019). Designing for task resumption support in mobile learning. Proceedings of the *21st International Conference on Human-Computer Interaction with Mobile Devices and Services*, 1–6. 10.1145/3338286.3344394

Engle, R.A., Langer-Osuna, J.M., & McKinney de Royston, M. (2014). Toward a model of influence in persuasive discussions: Negotiating quality, authority, privilege, and access within a student-led argument. *Journal of the Learning Sciences*, *23*(2), 245–268. 10.1080/10508406.2014.883979

Fozdar, B.I., & Kumar, L.S. (2007). Mobile learning and student retention. *International Review of Research in Open and Distance Learning*, *8*(2), 1–18.

Freeman, S., Eddy, S.L., McDonough, M., Smith, M.K., Okoroafor, N., Jordt, H., & Wenderoth, M.P. (2014). Active learning increases student performance in science, engineering, and mathematics. *Proceedings of the National Academy of Sciences*, *111*(23), 8410–8415. 10.1073/pnas.1319030111

Haak, D.C., HilleRisLambers, J., Pitre, E., & Freeman, S. (2011). Increased structure and active learning reduce the achievement gap in introductory biology. *Science*, *332*(6034), 1213–1216. 10.1126/science.1204820

Handelsman, J., Miller, S., & Pfund, C. (2007). *Scientific teaching*. Macmillan.

Kirschner, P.A., & De Bruyckere, P. (2017). The myths of the digital native and the multitasker. *Teaching and Teacher Education*, *67*, 135–142. 10.1016/j.tate.2017.06.001

Kuo-Hung, C., Kuo-En, C., Chung-Hsien, L., Kinshuk, & Yao-Ting, S. (2016). Integration of mobile AR technology in performance assessment. *Journal of Educational Technology & Society*, *19*(4), 239–251.

Ling, C., Harnish, D., & Shehab, R. (2014). Educational apps: Using mobile applications to enhance student learning of statistical concepts. *Human Factors and Ergonomics in Manufacturing & Service Industries*, *24*(5), 532–543. 10.1002/hfm.20550

Lorenzo, M., Crouch, C.H., & Mazur, E. (2006). Reducing the gender gap in the physics classroom. *American Journal of Physics*, *74*(2), 118–122. 10.1119/1.2162549

Nasser, R. (2014). Using mobile devices to increase student academic outcomes in Qatar. *Open Journal of Social Sciences*, 2(02), 67–73. 10.4236/jss.2014.22010

Nikou, S.A., & Economides, A.A. (2017). Mobile-based assessment: Investigating the factors that influence behavioral intention to use. *Computers & Education*, 109, 56–73. 10.1016/j.compedu.2017.02.005

Philip, T.M., & Gupta, A. (2020). Emerging perspectives on the co-construction of power and learning in the learning sciences, mathematics education, and science education. *Review of Research in Education*, 44(1), 195–217. 10.3102/0091732X20903

Prince, M. (2004). Does active learning work? A review of the research. *Journal of Engineering Education*, 93(3), 223–231. 10.1002/j.2168-9830.2004.tb00809.x

Ruiz-Primo, M.A., Briggs, D., Iverson, H., Talbot, R., & Shepard, L.A. (2011). Impact of undergraduate science course innovations on learning. *Science*, 331(6022), 1269–1270. 10.1126/science.1198976

Sauro, S. (2009). Strategic use of modality during synchronous CMC. *CALICO Journal*, 27(1), 101–117.

Sun, J.C.Y. (2014). Influence of polling technologies on student engagement: An analysis of student motivation, academic performance, and brainwave data. *Computers & Education*, 72, 80–89. 10.1016/j.compedu.2013.10.010

PART 4

I'VE DESIGNED MY MOBILE-FRIENDLY COURSE ... NOW WHAT?

9

PLAY!

UNDERSTANDING THE STUDENT EXPERIENCE

Reflect and iterate through play

I never thought I was "good" with technology. It all came to a head when I first started my PhD. I was struggling, trying to sync my notes on my iPad with my computer, and I couldn't figure it out. My first thought was I would ask my husband later that night to fix it for me. It struck me though that if I didn't empower myself with technology, I would struggle more and more. As technology would inevitably become more sophisticated and more integrated into our lives and work, I would just feel increasingly frustrated.

So I started playing around with technology. I realized the app I was trying to use for notes was not designed to sync across devices. Instead of trying to force the technology to do what it wasn't designed to do, I found an app that was designed to sync notes across devices. I started playing around with different features of my LMS, Canvas, like sending students individual messages. I created a digital cartoon for an assignment

DOI: 10.4324/9781003328773-13

in one of my classes. When I didn't understand a certain technology, I just spent a bit of time searching the internet for help articles. I began developing confidence that through play I could find ways to leverage technology in my learning, and I realized that I was not either "good" or "bad" at using technology. If there was something I didn't know how to do, I could figure it out. I had become empowered with technology through play. Now, when my daughter's iPad isn't working, she comes to me for help instead of my husband. And when my husband's phone isn't working, he often asks me what to do.

It is now more important than ever that we become empowered with using technology. New technologies emerge and both disrupt and transform our lives. Educators have seen classrooms change with the advent of personal computers, Microsoft Word, the internet, mobile devices, and artificial intelligence (AI) in the last 50 years alone. Although this list is not exhaustive, it can feel exhausting trying to keep up with these technologies. Adapting a sense of play can help us to become empowered in our own use of technology while we guide students in becoming mindful users of technology themselves. With the seemingly constant flow of emerging technologies, a sense of play will help us to design mobile-friendly courses and practice an approach that will empower us to use any emerging technology.

Mobile design principle #7: Play

Adopting a sense of play can help us to reflect and iterate to create more mobile-friendly courses. As instructors, we often design courses on computers, but students often access our courses on mobile devices (Baldwin & Ching, 2020). Given this disparity in design and use, we must adopt a sense of play to effectively gain an understanding and empathy for the student experience on mobile devices. A sense of play also aligns with the approach to mobile design as a journey. Our courses are not categorically mobile-friendly or not. There are aspects of our courses that are more mobile-friendly than others, and our pursuit of designing mobile-friendly courses is a journey. Given the ever-changing nature of mobile devices and mobile-friendly technologies, a sense of play will help us to not only grow as mobile designers, but also retain enthusiasm for the journey.

The following sections explore how we can approach mobile design through play by reflection and iteration. The strategies in these sections allow educators to adopt a sense of play to understand the student experience and make small changes to improve the mobile experience of our courses.

Playing through reflection

Reflection is foundational to our practice as educators. When I was getting my teaching credential, we were expected to write reflections after each lesson. Although this was certainly time-consuming, the practice of reflecting on what worked well and what I could improve on to better serve students has stuck with me. Reflection is also a crucial practice of equity-minded practitioners (Hammond, 2015; McNair et al., 2020). In mobile design, reflection can help us to approach the journey toward creating mobile-friendly courses with a sense of play. We don't have to be perfect from the start. Mobile design is not a skill that we learn once, but rather a journey in which we build an awareness of the benefits and limitations of mobile devices, the student experience, and the impacts of our course design on student learning.

To approach mobile design with a spirit of play through reflection, we can make it part of our process to view our courses on a mobile device. We can do this by downloading the app for our LMS if available. Then we can preview course content and assignments on the app to get a sense of the student experience. This simple approach can go a long way toward helping us to reflect on what it's like to access our courses on mobile devices.

We can also preview our courses on a mobile device without even leaving our computers. If we are interested in just seeing what our course looks like on a mobile device without leaving our computer, we can simply use keyboard shortcuts to preview what our course looks like on a mobile device. These keyboard shortcuts vary depending on the operating system (e.g., macOS or Windows) and the browser (e.g., Chrome or Firefox). An internet search can provide details on the specific keyboard shortcuts for a particular operating system and browser. When I use macOS and Chrome, I can press Option+Command+I. Then I can toggle between the phone and desktop preview (see Figure 9.1). When we see our course as it would appear on a mobile device, we might

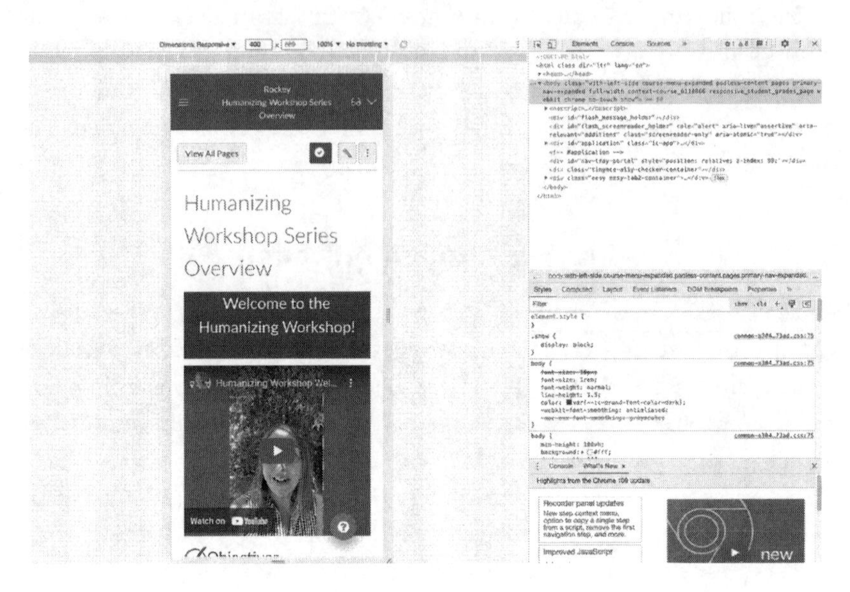

Figure 9.1 Keyboard shortcuts show a preview of our course on a mobile device without leaving our computer.

notice some small changes we could make to increase the mobile-friendliness of our course. For example, we may decide to add more headers if the text on a page is a little overwhelming on a small screen.

Another strategy we can use to play with mobile design is to try out apps or mobile-friendly tools before we use them in class. This is especially helpful as even seemingly mobile-friendly tools may not work in some circumstances. I have tried using tools I thought were mobile-friendly and found they did not work as planned. One such example occurred during an instructor workshop I facilitated. In this workshop, instructors and I were creating a toolkit of strategies we have used to humanize our classes. As the workshop was on Zoom, some instructors were joining from their phone. I shared a Google Doc and asked instructors to add their strategies to the Doc. However, some instructors found it difficult to read and contribute to the Google Doc with their small phone screen. Later in the session, we used Padlet, and everyone was able to add strategies to this board as it was easier to read and contribute to on a small screen. In this case, I had assumed that Google Docs was mobile-friendly. However, instructors struggled with adding their strategies and reading through their colleagues' strategies on a small phone screen. In contrast, Padlet chunked the content so it was easier for those using a phone to quickly skim through their colleagues' contributions. In this way, it is helpful to simply test out our activities on a mobile device so we can get a sense of the student experience.

To effectively reflect, we also need to get a sense of the student perspective. Providing mid-term surveys is an important component of reflective teaching and can provide an opportunity to gain insight into the mobile-friendliness of our courses. These surveys can also provide an opportunity for us to gain insight into how our students use mobile devices in their everyday lives. With a deeper understanding of how students already use mobile devices, we can tailor the design of our courses to align with students' use of phones.

In Chapter 7, we explored some sample survey questions that we could use at the beginning of the semester to gain an understanding of the tools that students use and to which they have access. Box 9.1 provides some questions we could ask in a mid-term survey:

BOX 9.1 MID-TERM SURVEY ON THE MOBILE STUDENT EXPERIENCE

1. I really like to use my phone to support my learning in this class by [check all that apply]:
   a. Watching and rewatching lectures
   b. Taking quizzes
   c. Completing assignments
   d. Reading for the course
   e. Other [fill in the blank]
2. I really don't like to use my phone to support my learning in this class by [check all that apply]:
   a. Watching and rewatching lectures
   b. Taking quizzes
   c. Completing assignments
   d. Reading for the course
   e. Other [fill in the blank]
3. I really like to use my phone to complete activities that take:
   a. Less than five minutes
   b. Less than ten minutes

   c. Less than 20 minutes
   d. Less than one hour
4. Is there anything else you would like to share about how you like to use your phone for learning in this course?
5. Are there any pages/activities that you can't complete on your phone that you would like to be able to use your phone to complete?
6. Are you able to use your phone for learning in other courses in ways that you would like to in this course? If so, please explain.

These questions can help us to gain insight into specific aspects of our courses that are particularly mobile-friendly as well as areas that we could make more mobile-friendly. The survey also provides us some insight into the aspects of the course that students like to be able to complete on their phone so we can prioritize our efforts in mobile design and spend our time on high-impact design moves.

After we have surveyed students on how they like to use their phones for learning, we can spend our time testing out our course in the way students use their phone. This helps us to prioritize our time. We don't need to spend time testing every aspect of our course on our phones if we know that students prefer to use their phones for specific tasks. The mid-term surveys may show that students prefer to use their phone to:

- join Zoom,
- take short quizzes,
- read an article, and
- watch a lecture video.

As such, we can spend time testing what it's like to use our phones to complete these tasks. Experiencing first-hand the tasks that students complete on a phone can help us to focus our reflection and make it less overwhelming to play with mobile design.

As educators, we are aware of the value of reflection. Reflection is foundational to our practice and equity-minded approaches to education (Hammond, 2015; McNair et al., 2020). In designing mobile-friendly courses, intentional reflection can help us to tailor our courses to best align with how students already use their phones for learning and how students would like to use their phones for learning. Reflection also helps us to embark on the journey of mobile-friendly design with a sense of play. Creating a mobile-friendly course can be a journey with an ever-changing finish line given the constant change of technologies. However, when we infuse our reflection with a sense of play, we can embark on the journey with joy and with a mindfulness of the value of our time.

Playing through iteration

Reflection can fall flat though if it doesn't prompt us to iterate on our practice. Reflection without iteration is like trying to bake bread without turning on the oven. When we pair reflection and iteration, we can adopt a sense of play as we embark on the journey of mobile design. The beauty of iteration is that we don't have to be perfect from the beginning. As we reflect, we can identify small changes we can make that will make a big difference for the mobile student experience.

First, we can make small changes to our course content to make it more mobile-friendly. As we reflect on the mobile experience and gather feedback from students, we can prioritize aspects of our course in which we will spend extra time to make it more mobile-friendly. Perhaps in our surveys with students, we discover many students prefer to use their phones to watch video lectures while commuting to work. In this case, we can iterate on the design of our course to create more short videos for students to watch while on a bus. We may also consider integrating short audio podcasts if we know many students drive to campus and would appreciate being able to use their commute to work through course content. We may also decide to focus our attention on double-duty strategies that help us meet accessibility guidelines. For example, students watching our lecture videos on the go may find that they are in noisy locations and would benefit from captions that are 100% accurate. Although we know the value of captions for accessibility purposes, we may also notice the value of captions for students who are using their phones on a noisy bus.

Second, we can make small changes to our assignments to make them more mobile-friendly. As we play with our assignments and gain a deeper understanding of the mobile student experience, we can iterate to make our courses more mobile-friendly. For example, we may notice that quizzes are especially easy to complete on a mobile device. As such, we may decide to leverage this tool more frequently to create more low-stakes opportunities for students to demonstrate their understanding of course concepts. We may also notice that certain assignments, like text-based discussions, are extremely difficult to scroll through on a mobile device. As such, we may decide to leverage a mobile-friendly tool to create video-based discussion posts.

As we iterate to create more mobile-friendly course content and assignments, we can also iterate on the directions that we provide to students. We may decide to revise directions after trying to complete an assignment on a mobile device. For example, we may notice that students will need to ensure they have an app downloaded before they start the assignment. We can make sure that we communicate this clearly. This is especially important for students who have smartphones but may have limited access to data on their phones. In this case, it will be important for students to know in advance that they need to download an app when they have access to WiFi.

Finally, we can empower students to share how they have leveraged their mobile devices for learning with future generations of students. As educators, we know that students love to hear from peers, but peer-to-peer learning also provides a powerful opportunity for learning (Tullis & Goldstone, 2020). Although smartphone ownership is nearly ubiquitous (Pew Research Center, 2021), students often have more practice using their phones for their personal lives than as a tool for learning (Kirschner & De Bruyckere, 2017). Students may have also internalized pervasive K–12 bans on phones in the classroom and may need permission to feel comfortable using their phones for learning in the classroom. As such, one powerful way we can iterate on our mobile design is to ask students to share with future generations of students how they successfully used their phones to support their learning in our course. By sharing these tips and tricks, students will not only offer advice to their peers, but they will also offer helpful insight that we can use to iterate on our course design. If we notice that many students use their phones to communicate with peers via the class Discord, we may decide to make small changes to our course to ensure that all students are aware of this resource.

As we reflect, we also need to iterate. Making small changes to our course content and assignments can help to prioritize our time on revisions that will have the biggest impact on how our students use mobile devices for learning in our courses. Revising directions will also help us to support students as they use mobile devices for learning in our courses. Finally, we can empower students to share how they use their phones for learning. This will help us to support students as they themselves explore how to leverage mobile devices for their learning. By continuously iterating on our courses, we can make small changes to our course design that can have a big impact on how students experience our courses on their phones.

A journey of play

Reflection and iteration can help us to continuously tailor our courses to best serve our students. Although research provides helpful recommendations for mobile-friendly course design, depending on our student populations and our local context, we may find that there may be important variations in how students prefer to use their phones. For example, if we teach a course in which many of the students are parents of young children, we'll likely want to focus more energy on creating chunks of content so students can work through the course in the found moments of their day. If we teach a course in a rural area where students do not have access to reliable internet in their homes, we will likely want to focus on creating content that can be downloaded or accessed easily via a mobile device so students can use their mobile devices to work on course content outside of the class. We may also find that our students may not have access to affordable internet on their phones, and as such, we'll want to make sure that content can be downloaded and phones can be leveraged for learning offline. By approaching mobile design with a sense of play, we can truly adopt the approach that it is not an either/or, but rather a journey. In this chapter, we explored the following strategies for approaching mobile design through a lens of play (Box 9.2):

BOX 9.2 MOBILE DESIGN IN ACTION

Play!

- Playing through Reflection
  - View your course on a mobile device
  - Try out apps before you use them in class

  - Survey students to generate a better understanding of their mobile experience
  - Test out the aspects of your course students like to use a phone to complete
- Playing through Iteration
  - Make small changes to your course content to make it more mobile-friendly
  - Make small changes to your assignments to make them more mobile-friendly
  - Revise directions for students to make activities easier to complete on their phones
  - Empower students to share how they use their mobile devices for the course

By reflecting and iterating on the mobile experience of our courses, we can make small changes that have an outsized impact on how students are able to leverage their phones to complete coursework. Adopting a spirit of play in our reflection and iteration process can help us to recognize that mobile design is not an either/or. Instead, we can make small changes that help us to better serve students in our mobile course design journey to transform access to higher education while acting ourselves as empowered users of technology (Box 9.3).

BOX 9.3 REFLECTION

Now let's take a moment to reflect on these strategies. Which of these strategies are already part of your practice? Which of these strategies do you commit to making part of your practice when reflecting and iteracting on your course design? Take a moment to set an intention to choose one or two strategies that you will begin implementing tomorrow. Taking steps to implement more of these strategies can have a big impact on how students can leverage mobile devices for learning.

References

Baldwin, S.J., & Ching, Y.H. (2020). Guidelines for designing online courses for mobile devices. *TechTrends*, 64(3), 413–422.

Hammond, Z. (2015). *Culturally responsive teaching and the brain: Promoting authentic engagement and rigor among culturally and linguistically diverse students*. Corwin Press.

Kirschner, P.A., & De Bruyckere, P. (2017). The myths of the digital native and the multitasker. *Teaching and Teacher Education*, 67, 135–142. 10.1016/j.tate.2017.06.001

McNair, T.B., Bensimon, E.M., & Malcom-Piqueux, L. (2020). *From equity talk to equity walk: Expanding practitioner knowledge for racial justice in higher education*. John Wiley & Sons.

Pew Research Center (2021). Mobile fact sheet. https://www.pewresearch.org/internet/fact-sheet/mobile/

Tullis, J.G., & Goldstone, R.L. (2020). Why does peer instruction benefit student learning?. *Cognitive Research: Principles and Implications*, 5(1), 1–12. 10.1186/s41235-020-00218-5

10

COMMUNICATE

ADVERTISING MOBILE-FRIENDLINESS

Setting a campus-wide tone

Many of our students may have access to and use a smartphone for personal use daily, but students need guidance on how to use mobile devices for learning (Kirschner & De Bruyckere, 2017). Given persistent bans on mobile devices in K–16 classrooms (Jones et al., 2020), students may even have internalized the perspective that their smartphone is a distraction and not a tool for learning. However, many students will use their mobile devices in future careers (Harris & Greer, 2021; Narayan, et al., 2019). Students need guidance and practice on using their phones for learning and for professional purposes. This also provides students an opportunity to practice ways in which they can manage the pull of mobile devices on their attention (Barden & Bygroves, 2018). By providing opportunities for students to use their mobile devices for learning, we give students a chance to learn how to leverage this tool for learning purposes while managing the distractibility factor.

DOI: 10.4324/9781003328773-14

Mobile design principle #8: Communicate

Both instructors and institutions play an important role in communicating to students a sense that mobile devices can be a tool for learning. Instructors can communicate to students the mobile-friendliness of their course and indicate to students when and how they can use their phone for learning. Institutions can create opportunities for grassroots mobile-friendly movements to flourish across campus. Institutions can also focus on ways in which mobile-friendly systems can create a campus culture that is inclusive and welcoming of mobile devices.

The following sections explore how we can communicate the mobile-friendliness of our courses as instructors as well as institutions. When instructors and institutions work in conjunction to communicate an acceptance of mobile devices, we can set a campus-wide tone that encourages the use of mobile devices for learning and helps to reduce some of the stigma students may have internalized with persistent K–16 bans on phones in classrooms (Jones et al., 2020).

Communicating mobile-friendliness as an instructor

As educators, we can help to establish a mobile-friendly tone in our courses. We can encourage the use of phones for learning by explicitly communicating the mobile-friendliness of our courses and implying an acceptance of mobile devices for learning. For many of our students, their phones are a "lifeline to education" (Baldwin & Ching, 2020, p. 420). Students may need to use phones for learning because:

- they don't have access to internet at home,
- they share a computer with multiple members of their family,
- their computer is old and slow to turn on, and/or
- they need to make use of small chunks of their day after they drop off kids at school or when they're on a break at work.

Due to continued bans on mobile devices (Jones et al., 2020), students may have internalized a sense that phones should not be used for learning. Students may also feel that a phone is not as good as a computer, and they may feel a sense of embarrassment for not having internet in their home or a functioning personal computer. A mobile-friendly tone in our courses can create an environment in which students use their phones not because they don't have access to computers, but to make use of the unique benefits of mobile devices for learning. In this way, we are reframing mobile devices as an asset and not a deficit. We can communicate to students the value of phones for learning and move away from a deficit perspective that students who rely on mobile devices for learning are at a disadvantage.

One of the first places we can communicate the mobile-friendliness of our courses is in the syllabus. We can clearly explain how students can use their mobile devices to work through course content and which assignments they might need to use a computer to complete. This will provide students the chance to arrange access to a computer or to plan what times of the semester they may need childcare to be able to complete some assignments at the library.

We can also use our syllabus to imply an acceptance of mobile devices by creating a version of our syllabus that students can easily access on a mobile device. Pacansky-Brock's (2017) liquid syllabus is a mobile-friendly version of our syllabus that is created on a website. The liquid syllabus provides a foundation upon which students can get to know us through friendly welcome videos and our course through success kits that demystify how to be successful in the first week of the course (Pacansky-Brock, 2017). As the liquid syllabus is designed to be more accessible on the small screen of a phone than a traditional PDF syllabus, it is also a great strategy to set a mobile-friendly tone for our class.

Welcome emails provide an opportunity to explicitly communicate the mobile-friendliness of our courses. Many instructors will send students a welcome email a week before the start of the course with important information about the course. This welcome email is a perfect place to describe how students can use their phones for course content and assignments. The following example provides a sample welcome email (Box 10.1):

BOX 10.1 SAMPLE WELCOME EMAIL

Hello Class!

Thank you for enrolling in [NAME OF COURSE]. My name is Dr. Alex Rockey (you can call me Alex), and I will be your instructor this semester. Our official start date for this course is [DATE], but I wanted to take a moment to share some helpful tips to make sure you start the semester off strong.

1. ***Log in to [name of LMS] to view our course.*** *All your assignments and readings will be posted on our [name of LMS] course. The course is organized with a module for each week.*
2. ***Download the [name of LMS] app.*** *Good news! You can complete [all/some/most] of the course on your phone! Before the class starts, take a moment to download the [name of LMS] app on your phone so you'll be ready to work on the course anytime/anywhere!*
3. ***Read the syllabus.*** *The syllabus provides a helpful overview of the assignments and readings you'll complete in this course. Before the first day of class, be sure to read through the syllabus (attached) to get a sense of the work you'll be completing in this course. The syllabus also indicates the assignments for which you'll need access to a computer. This is to help you plan ahead for assignments that will be difficult to complete on your phone.*
4. *ADD ANY OTHER TIPS*

I am excited to work with you this semester! If you have any questions, please don't hesitate to reach out.

See you next week!

Alex

By clearly communicating to students how they can use their phones for learning in the welcome email, we can set a mobile-friendly tone for our course even before the course begins.

We can also develop systems to communicate the mobile-friendliness of course content or assignments as students work through the course. In Chapter 5, we discussed adding images to pages to indicate the mobile-friendliness of course content. We can also consider ways in which we can communicate the mobile-friendliness of assignments or course content for the whole course at a glance. Some LMSs may allow us to place emojis within a module so students can quickly see which pages and assignments are mobile-friendly. Figure 10.1 provides an example of symbols in a module in Canvas. The phone symbols indicate aspects of the course that are mobile-friendly, whereas the computer indicates assignments/course content in which students would benefit from using a computer.

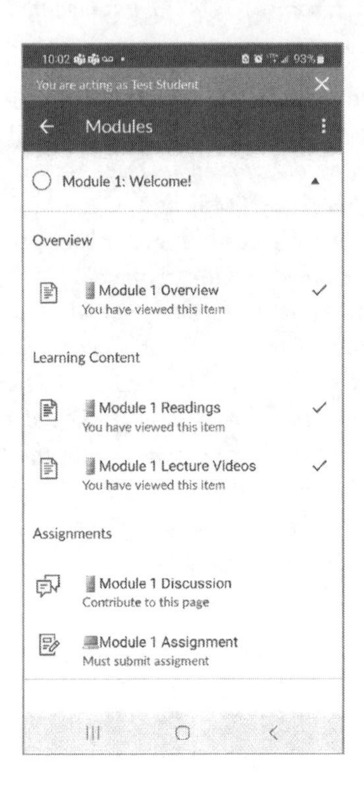

Figure 10.1 Symbols can show students mobile-friendly pages at a glance.

Creating a consistent system to indicate to students when they can use their phones for learning can help to counteract student perceptions that phones are not meant to be used for learning. If we decide to use symbols to indicate the mobile-friendliness of course content and assignments, we can communicate this in our syllabus and our welcome email to ensure students know from the beginning of the course what these symbols mean. Depending on if we teach face-to-face or online, we can also explain this in one of our first class sessions or create a short video highlighting the symbols and how students can use them to know when to leverage their phones for learning.

Leveraging mobile-friendly tools for course content like embedded videos or podcasts implies an acceptance of mobile devices for learning. Many students will try to use their mobile devices for courses, but quickly abandon the pursuit as courses are typically not designed to be accessed or completed on mobile devices. As such, students may get frustrated and decide to use a computer to complete coursework instead. However, when we leverage mobile-friendly tools to deliver course content, we can encourage students to use their phones for learning in our courses.

We can also use mobile-friendly tools for assignments. These assignments can be formative, low-stakes assignments in class with tools like Mentimeter, Kahoot!, Padlet, or Jamboard. The benefit of using mobile-friendly tools is that many of these tools include directions that work for both computers and mobile devices. For example, Kahoot! will automatically display directions for students to log in to the Kahoot! via a computer or the app. Using these tools implies an acceptance of mobile devices.

As instructors, we need to ensure that we indicate how students can use mobile devices in our courses. By communicating to students ways in which they can use mobile devices for learning, we can reframe the use of mobile devices for learning as a positive and help to move away from a deficit perspective.

Communicating mobile-friendliness as an institution

Colleges and universities can support the work of instructors to create mobile-friendly courses by providing opportunities for grassroots mobile-friendly movements to grow and by creating mobile-friendly institutional systems. By working with centers for teaching and learning, offices of institutional research, offices of student life, admissions, and academic technology, colleges and universities can leverage the expertise on campus to create mobile-friendly institutions that communicate to students an acceptance of mobile devices for learning.

As institutions, colleges and universities can provide opportunities for grassroots mobile-friendly movements to grow across campus. First, professional development and centers for teaching and learning can create faculty learning communities for instructors on campus. Faculty learning communities provide instructors an opportunity to talk about and reflect on teaching and learning in collaboration with colleagues (Cross, 1998; Shapiro & Levine, 1999; Ward & Selvester, 2012). Faculty learning communities help to support professional development and hold a powerful potential to transform teaching practices (Ward & Selvester, 2012). Given the collaborative and reflective nature of faculty learning communities, instructors can experience profound growth as educators compared to the more passive learning experience typically encountered during one-off workshops (Ward & Selvester, 2012). Just as students love to hear from students, instructors love to hear from other instructors. Faculty learning communities align with the approach to mobile design as a journey. Creating mobile-friendly courses is not an either/or, but rather a journey in which we continuously iterate and reflect. Participating in faculty learning communities on mobile design can help instructors to find colleagues to collaborate with as they embark on the mobile design journey.

Offices of institutional research can also help to build an awareness of the local context and how students on campus use mobile devices for learning and for personal purposes. Surveying students on ways in which they use mobile learning can have a profound impact on how instructors can design mobile-friendly courses. For example, if students on a particular campus do not frequently have access to internet in their home and don't have unlimited data, instructors may want to ensure that courses require little data and may limit extraneous images that take extra data to load. Instructors may also be careful to ensure that students can download videos when they have access to WiFi to support learning without straining data plans.

Universities can also work with centers for student life to showcase students who have learned how to use their phones in creative ways to make progress on schoolwork. Although students often use mobile devices for personal purposes, they need guidance on ways in which they can use phones for learning (Kirschner & De Bruyckere, 2017). By showcasing examples of students who have learned how to leverage their phones for learning, offices of student life can not only set a tone of mobile-friendliness at an institutional level, but they can also inspire students to make use of their phones for learning.

In addition to supporting grassroots movements, colleges and universities can work to create mobile-friendly institutional systems in coordination with admissions and academic technology. First, institutions can work to create mobile-friendly registration processes. Although this is no small task, registration is often one of the first experiences students will have with a college or university. Creating mobile-friendly registration processes can communicate to students that they are welcome to use their phones for learning at the college or university. Dedicating time and effort to creating mobile-friendly registration processes is especially important for open access institutions where any student can enroll. Registration processes can sometimes be tedious, lengthy, confusing, and in conflict with the mission of open access institutions. As such, redesigning the registration process to be mobile-friendly will benefit not only students who rely on their phones, but also all students who appreciate a more streamlined process to enroll.

Once students have enrolled in a college or university, institutions can create a system to communicate to students the mobile-friendliness of courses. This could begin as a grassroots movement and could be as simple as a website highlighting the courses on campus that are mobile-friendly. However, as more courses become mobile-friendly across campus, institutions could create a system that indicates to students the mobile-friendliness of a course when they register for specific classes. Having this information when registering is important for students who may depend on their mobile device for learning, but it also helps to communicate and set an institutional tone of acceptance for mobile devices for learning. Just as we communicate to students when a course uses a "Zero Cost Textbook," we can also create a symbol to communicate to students the mobile-friendliness of a particular course.

Academic technology departments also have an important role to play in supporting instructors on their mobile design journey and communicating to students a general acceptance of mobile devices for learning. One place to start is by demonstrating a mindfulness of the mobile-friendliness of tools before adopting a site-wide license. In my role as a faculty in the academic technology department, I have been part of many calls regarding new tools for which we have considered adopting a site-wide license. In these calls, I always make sure to ask if students will be able to use their phone to access the tool. I have been shocked by the response from the sales reps. In one such call, the sales rep said students shouldn't use their phone for learning and the tool wouldn't be very easy to use on a phone. I was shocked by the disregard the sales rep showed for how our students use phones for learning and the lack of consideration for our students who rely on their mobile devices to succeed in their courses. By incorporating attention to the mobile-friendliness of tools when adopting site-wide licenses, departments of academic technology can not only communicate to students that mobile devices should be allowed to be used for learning, but also communicate to companies the importance of considering this aspect of student use when designing their tools.

Finally, departments of academic technology can make sure that their LMS is mobile-friendly. Although many LMSs offer mobile apps, some LMSs are not easy to use on a phone. Changing LMSs is a Herculean task, but if an institution is making a move from one LMS to another, the mobile-friendliness of the LMS needs to be an important consideration.

Institutions can help to set the tone on a campus and communicate to students a general acceptance of mobile devices for learning. By including institutions in the mobile design journey, we can help to:

- prompt more faculty to embark on the mobile design journey,
- tailor mobile design to our specific student populations and local needs,
- inspire students to use mobile devices for learning through student showcases,
- reenvision registration processes to be inclusive of mobile devices, and
- ensure the tools our campus uses are mobile-friendly.

Each of these strategies helps to communicate an institutional commitment to mobile-friendly course design. By leveraging the expertise of departments across campus to support mobile-friendly course design, we can create mobile-friendly institutions that can have a profound impact on communicating an acceptance of mobile devices and help students to view their phones as tools for learning.

Instructors and institutions: Working in concert to set a tone of mobile inclusivity

Mobile devices can be powerful tools for learning. However, students need guidance on how they can use mobile devices for learning (Kirschner & De Bruyckere, 2017). With continued bans on phones in K–16 classrooms (Jones et al., 2020), students may have internalized a sense that mobile devices should not be used for learning. Although some students rely on their mobile devices to be successful in their courses, all students can benefit from leveraging the powerful tools in their pockets for anytime/anywhere learning. As such, an important step on the mobile-friendly course design journey is to communicate to students how and when they can use their mobile devices for learning. When instructors and institutions make a concerted effort to communicate to students how to use mobile devices for learning, they can make strides toward creating a campus culture that is inclusive and welcoming of mobile devices.

In this chapter, we explored the following strategies to communicate mobile-friendliness (Box 10.2):

BOX 10.2 MOBILE DESIGN IN ACTION

COMMUNICATE!

- Communicating Mobile-Friendliness as an Instructor
  - Describe how students can use their phones for learning in the syllabus
  - Create a mobile-friendly syllabus
  - Send a welcome email to explain the mobile-friendliness of a course
  - Establish systems to indicate mobile-friendly assignments or course content
  - Use mobile-friendly tools
- Communicating Mobile-Friendliness as an Institution
  - Develop faculty learning communities on mobile-friendly course design
  - Build awareness of local student uses of mobile devices for learning
  - Showcase students who make use of phones for learning
  - Create mobile-friendly registration processes
  - Create an institution-wide system for communicating mobile-friendly courses
  - Ensure tools are mobile-friendly before committing to a site-wide license
  - Adopt mobile-friendly LMSs

Setting a campus-wide tone that communicates acceptance of mobile devices for learning combines both explicit and implicit communication on the part of the instructor and supports grassroots movements and reenvisioning systems on the part of the institution. Students need to see how they can use their mobile devices for learning at a course level, but they also need to experience institutions that are inclusive of phones through systems like mobile-friendly registration processes. As instructors we can do our part by communicating the mobile-friendly aspects of our courses to students. We can also support institutional efforts that bring together departments across campus to highlight the work instructors and students are already doing to leverage mobile devices for learning. When institutional systems align with our work as instructors, we can set a campus-wide tone that doesn't just tolerate phones, but instead celebrates the use of mobile devices for learning (Box 10.3).

BOX 10.3 REFLECTION

Now let's take a moment to reflect on these strategies. Which of these strategies are already part of your practice? Which of these strategies do you commit to making part of your practice when communicating to students? Take a moment to set an intention to choose one or two strategies that you will begin implementing tomorrow. Taking steps to implement more of these strategies can have a big impact on the mobile-friendly tone of a course and of the campus as a whole.

References

Baldwin, S.J., & Ching, Y.H. (2020). Guidelines for designing online courses for mobile devices. *TechTrends*, *64*(3), 413–422.

Barden, O., & Bygroves, M. (2018). 'I wouldn't be able to graduate if it wasn't for my mobile phone.' The affordances of mobile devices in the construction of complex academic texts. *Innovations in Education and Teaching International*, *55*(5), 555–565. 10.1080/14703297.2017.1322996

Cross, K.P. (1998). Classroom research: Implementing the scholarship of teaching. *New Directions for Teaching and Learning*, *75*, 5–12. 10.1002/tl.7501

Harris, H.S., & Greer, M. (2021). Using multimedia for instructor presence in purposeful pedagogy-driven online technical writing courses. *Journal of Technical Writing and Communication*, 51(1), 31–52. 10.1177/004728162 0977162

Jones, S.B., Aruguete, M.S., & Gretlein, R. (2020). Cell phone use policies in the college classroom: Do they work?. *Transactions of the Missouri Academy of Science*, *48*(2020), 5–9. 10.30956/MAS-31R1

Kirschner, P.A., & De Bruyckere, P. (2017). The myths of the digital native and the multitasker. *Teaching and Teacher Education*, *67*, 135–142. 10.1016/ j.tate.2017.06.001

Narayan, V., Herrington, J., & Cochrane, T. (2019). Design principles for heutagogical learning: Implementing student-determined learning with mobile and social media tools. *Australasian Journal of Educational Technology*, *35*(3). 10.14742/ajet.3941

Pacansky-Brock, M. (2017). *Best practices for teaching with emerging technologies* (2nd edition). Routledge.

Shapiro, N.S., & Levine, J.H. (1999). *Creating learning communities: A practical guide to winning support, organizing for change, and implementing programs*. Jossey-Bass.

Ward, H.C., & Selvester, P.M. (2012). Faculty learning communities: Improving teaching in higher education. *Educational Studies*, *38*(1), 111–121. 10.1080/ 03055698.2011.567029

PART

5

WHAT'S THE FUTURE OF MOBILE DESIGN?

11

SUPPORT YOUR COLLEAGUES

A TOOLKIT FOR INSTRUCTOR SUPPORT

Embarking on the journey together

Throughout my time in education, I have heard one saying repeatedly: "Educators make the worst students." I heard this saying from colleagues when we were attending workshops at the district when I taught high school English. And I heard this saying from workshop participants during my time offering professional development at the college level. In my experience, I don't think this saying is true. Students and teachers alike want learning experiences that are meaningful and applicable to their lives. Students and teachers are both learners, and any learner wants to engage in learning experiences for which they can see real-world applications. Teachers just may be a bit more vocal (at least to their colleagues) when a workshop or course doesn't help them better serve their students.

Effective professional development inspires and transforms. Darling-Hammond et al. (2017) in a review of 35 studies on effective professional development found seven characteristics were shared in effective

DOI: 10.4324/9781003328773-16

professional development opportunities. They found high-quality professional development:

1. Focuses on content
2. Includes active learning
3. Promotes collaboration
4. Models good teaching
5. Utilizes coaching
6. Includes feedback
7. Extends over a period of time (Darling-Hammond et al., 2017).

Darling-Hammond et al. (2017) noted that high-quality professional development includes most, if not all, of these seven characteristics.

Effective professional development can have transformative impacts on an educator's practice as well as student learning outcomes (Darling-Hammond et al., 2017). However, the potential of professional development to improve the teaching and learning experience is not always realized. Too often professional development workshops do not model the pedagogical approaches (e.g., active learning) educators are encouraged to adopt in their classrooms. As educators, we all likely have experienced professional development workshops that focus more on a list of to-dos and less on "iterative and thoughtful reflection on practice" (Mellow et al., 2015, p. 10). As mobile-friendly course design is a reflective journey, workshops to guide educators in leveraging mobile devices for learning will naturally focus on adopting a reflective approach to course design.

As we consider ways in which we can support our colleagues in developing as mobile-friendly course designers, this chapter will present four workshop outlines that incorporate opportunities for active learning, collaboration, and coaching. These workshops also model effective use of mobile-friendly tools for engagement and extend over a period of time. Educators deserve quality professional development that inspires, promotes reflection, supports a sense of growth, and applies to local contexts. Through quality professional development, we can support educators as they embark on the mobile design journey to reduce barriers of access and change students' lives.

Workshop outlines

These four workshop outlines can be reworked to best meet the timeline and unique context in which they are delivered. The workshops include goals that detail the learning outcomes. In addition, each workshop includes ideas for ways to model mobile use and adopt the workshop to a local context. The workshops include activity suggestions as well as an outline of topics to cover. Each of the parts of this book can provide content for the outlines. Each of the workshops is meant to span 90 minutes but can be adopted for shorter chunks or longer chunks as needed. The workshops can be offered virtually, face to face, or some combination of the two. These outlines provide a starting point that can be adopted in limitless ways to best serve specific contexts, timeframes, and participant needs.

Workshop #1: Why does mobile design matter?

In this interactive workshop, participants will work to answer the question "Why Does Mobile Design Matter?" They will reflect on their own mobile device use as well as how they imagine students use mobile devices in their personal lives. Participants will also analyze one of their courses and determine where it falls on the mobile-friendly course continuum in terms of course content and assignments. Finally, participants will explore the benefits and limitations of mobile devices. The workshop will conclude with a look forward to the next session on designing mobile-friendly course content.

Goals

1. Discuss why mobile design can make use of how students already use phones in their personal lives.
2. Discuss why mobile design can reduce barriers of access.
3. Understand benefits and limitations of mobile devices.
4. Reflect on where a particular course falls on the mobile-friendly course continuum in terms of course content and assignments.

Model mobile use

To model mobile use in this workshop, consider sharing the slides for the workshop with a QR code and a bit.ly so instructors can access and follow along on their phones. You can also consider using mobile-friendly tools (e.g., Mentimeter or Poll Everywhere) to gather and display responses on mobile device use. Finally, when instructors analyze where their course falls on the course continuum, they can share this analysis on a digital whiteboard (e.g., Jamboard). Just be mindful to not include too many different tools as there may be a learning curve for each tool. As you consider using tools, be considerate of instructor comfort level with technology.

Make it local

To make it local, consider pulling in data on how students use mobile devices or how many students rely on mobile devices for internet on your campus. Some campuses may have access to data that demonstrates which device and operating system students use to access the LMS. This can help to inform mobile design approaches as you may find that students are overwhelmingly using a particular device to access the LMS at your institution (Table 11.1).

Workshop outline

Table 11.1 Workshop #1 outline.

Agenda	*Activity Suggestions*
Introduction a. Welcome b. Discuss goals c. Review agenda d. Get to know each other	To get to know each other, ask instructors to reflect and share on how frequently and for what purposes they use their mobile devices. Ask instructors to reflect and share how frequently and for what purposes their students use their mobile devices. This could be a think-pair-share or a full group discussion.
Consider Our Learners a. Designing for use i. Discuss how students use their mobile devices in their lives	Ask instructors to reflect on students who rely on mobile devices for learning and consider ways in which mobile devices can be leveraged to reduce barriers of access.

(continued on next page)

Table 11.1 (Continued)

Agenda	*Activity Suggestions*
b. Reducing barriers of access i. Creating access regardless of home internet ii. Creating global learning experiences iii. Serving the so-called nontraditional student iv. Supporting students experiencing disruptions	
The Mobile-Friendly Course Continuum a. Reflect on the mobile-friendly course continuum b. Discuss the benefits of mobile devices c. Discuss the limitations of mobile devices	Introduce mobile-friendly course design as a journey that allows us to move along a continuum to continuously work to create more mobile-friendly courses. Ask instructors to reflect on a course and where it falls on the mobile-friendly course continuum. Instructors can then indicate on a digital whiteboard (e.g., Jamboard) where their course content and assignments fall on the continuum. Discuss the benefits and limitations of mobile devices.
Wrap Up a. Mobile-friendly course design as a journey b. Looking forward: Creating mobile-friendly course content	Reiterate mobile design as a journey and introduce the next workshop focus: Creating mobile-friendly course content. Consider integrating a tool to facilitate communication among workshop participants between workshops to share questions/thoughts on mobile-friendly course design.

Workshop #2: How do I design content students can access on their phones?

Creating mobile-friendly course content can feel overwhelming. To move away from a list of to-dos, this interactive workshop will work to answer the question "How Do I Design Content Students Can Access on Their Phones?" Participants will explore guiding principles for designing mobile-friendly course content that focus on how we can create content for small screens, build trust, and leverage moments. For each of these principles, educators will review strategies to enact these principles. Then educators will choose two to four strategies they will apply to their own courses and work in small groups to make these changes to their courses. Instructors will share screenshots of their revised course content and discuss as a larger group the impact these changes have on the mobile-friendliness of their course. This workshop will conclude with a reflection in which instructors set an intention for further revisions they will make to their course.

Goals

1. Apply two to four strategies for designing content for small screens to create mobile-friendly course content.
2. Apply two to four strategies for building trust to create mobile-friendly course content.
3. Apply two to four strategies for leveraging moments to create mobile-friendly course content.
4. Reflect on experience enacting strategies and set goals for designing mobile-friendly course content.

Model mobile use

As we model mobile use, we want to continue to be mindful of not introducing too many new tools. For this reason, it would be helpful to continue using the same mobile-friendly tools chosen in the first workshop. In this workshop, we can model mobile by simply providing space for educators to showcase their course content through screenshots taken on their phone. The more we are able to see and experience our courses on mobile devices, the more we will be able to build an intuition for mobile-friendly design.

Make it local

To make it local, consider including statistics or quotes that reflect students on your particular campus. As instructors, there is really nothing more powerful than hearing the student voice. When discussing building trust, highlighting specific data or quotes from your student population on smartphone dependency can bring the importance of trust to life.

When discussing leveraging moments, it can be helpful to pull in statistics or student voices that help educators more deeply understand what it's like for students who are balancing jobs, childcare, elder care, or commutes (Table 11.2).

Workshop outline

Table 11.2 Workshop outline #2.

Agenda	*Activity Suggestions*
Introduction a. Welcome b. Discuss goals c. Review agenda	If a tool was used to facilitate communication between workshop sessions, consider allocating some time to address frequent questions/thoughts on mobile design discussed between sessions.
Create Content for Small Screens a. Chunking content i. Use modules to organize course content ii. Add text headers to modules iii. Add headers to pages iv. Use accordions or tabs b. Creating a visually appealing and accessible experience i. Avoid tables ii. Use responsive images iii. Move content directly into the LMS iv. Use descriptive hyperlinks v. Use Sans Serif fonts and 14-point font vi. Avoid indenting vii. Use bold (not italics) for emphasis	To help instructors focus on the guiding principles (and to not feel overwhelmed by a list of to-dos), provide opportunities for participants to experience course content that is designed to maximize small screens on their phones. Provide instructors an overview of how we can create content for small screens by chunking content and creating visually appealing pages. Then, poll instructors to determine if anyone would like a tutorial on how to implement any of the strategies in their courses. Guide instructors through tutorials as needed. Assign instructors to small groups, and ask the groups to choose two to four strategies they will apply to their own courses. Ask instructors to submit a screenshot of a page to a virtual whiteboard (e.g., Jamboard) to showcase their work. Wrap up this section with a brief discussion as a full group on what instructors learned about designing content for small screens but keep instructors in small groups for the next section.

(*continued on next page*)

Table 11.2 (Continued)

Agenda	*Activity Suggestions*
Build Trust a. Showing care through consistency i. Simplify navigation ii. Keep navigation consistent iii. Ensure navigation is clear b. Demonstrate understanding by removing wait times i. Avoid requiring students to download files ii. Remove unnecessary images iii. Be mindful of file sizes of images iv. Limit unnecessary clicks c. Communicating acceptance by designing for touch screens i. Create directions that work regardless of device ii. Embed videos directly into the page iii. Hyperlink email addresses and phone numbers	Discuss the power of mobile devices for building trust and how we can show care through consistency and communicate acceptance by designing for touch screens. Take time to gauge if participants need tutorials on how to hyperlink email addresses and phone numbers or how to ensure file sizes are not too large for mobile devices. Consider polling instructors again to see if any tutorials are needed. Ask instructors again to work in their small groups to prioritize two to four strategies to apply to their own courses. Have instructors submit screenshots to another virtual whiteboard (e.g., Jamboard) and wrap up this section with a brief group discussion.
Leverage Moments a. Creating content in ten-minute chunks i. Chunk content into quick tasks ii. Keep pages short (less than 2,000 words) b. Designing for stops and starts i. Create a consistent way to communicate mobile-friendly course content ii. Encourage students to turn on some notifications and turn off others iii. Design for how students use the LMS on their phone iv. Add completion requirements	Ask instructors to reflect on how they use mobile devices in the in-between parts of their day. Discuss the power of these small chunks of time for students who are balancing childcare, work, commutes, and/or elder care. Provide instructors a chance to request tutorials on specific strategies for leveraging moments. In small groups, ask instructors again to prioritize two to four strategies and apply in their own courses. Provide a digital whiteboard in which instructors can submit screenshots to highlight their work and how they made their course content more mobile-friendly. Wrap up with a brief discussion.
Wrap Up a. Looking forward: Creating mobile-friendly assignments	Provide a space for instructors to reflect on their work today and set intentions for next steps. Instructors can reflect on the following questions:

(continued on next page)

Table 11.2 (Continued)

Agenda	*Activity Suggestions*
	1. What did you find most useful in creating mobile-friendly course content? 2. What did you struggle with in creating mobile-friendly course content? 3. What will you implement in your courses today (or tomorrow) to make course content more mobile-friendly? Give a brief preview of the next session on creating mobile-friendly assignments.

Workshop #3: How do I design assignments students can complete on their phones?

By designing mobile-friendly assignments, we can reduce barriers of access for our students and help to move our courses towards being more mobile-friendly. This interactive workshop will guide participants through the redesign of one assignment to become more mobile-friendly by allowing choice, integrating multimodality, and leveraging mobile-friendly tools. The workshop will conclude with a reflection of the changes instructors made to their assignment as well as takeaways that they will apply to other assignments.

Goals

1. Create a mobile-friendly assignment that allows choice and leverages mobile-friendly tools.
2. Integrate multimodality into an assignment OR create a survey to better understand how comfortable students are with using tools needed for creating multimodal content.

Model mobile use

One section of this workshop focuses on leveraging mobile-friendly tools to design mobile-friendly assignments. We can model mobile use by providing opportunities for instructors to interact with the mobile-friendly tools throughout this workshop and previous workshops. We can consider integrating short polls or quizzes with tools like Kahoot!, Poll Everywhere, or Google Forms. Another option could be to create interactive experiences for participants via augmented reality through games like Pokémon Go.

Make it local

As one portion of this workshop focuses on making use of the LMS, it would be helpful to tailor this section to the LMS used on campus. Providing recommendations and examples specific to the localized instance of the LMS will help to make use of the specific teaching context in which instructors will be enacting mobile-friendly principles (Table 11.3).

Workshop outline

Table 11.3 Workshop #3 outline.

Agenda	*Activity Suggestions*
Introduction a. Welcome b. Complete assignment on mobile device c. Discuss goals d. Review agenda	Begin the session by having instructors complete an assignment on their phone. This could be a discussion post, or this could be a quiz. Choose an assignment type that is commonly used on your campus. Then ask instructors to participate in a think-pair-share in which they reflect on their experience. What worked well (if anything) when submitting an assignment on their phone? What challenges did they face? Then introduce the principles for designing mobile-friendly assignments. Ask instructors to choose one assignment to design in which they can allow choice, integrate multimodality, and leverage mobile-friendly tools.

(continued on next page)

Table 11.3 (Continued)

Agenda	*Activity Suggestions*
Allow Choice a. Providing choice in device type i. Let students take a picture of assignments and upload ii. Write directions that work for any medium b. Grading content, not device i. Focus on the outcomes not on the device ii. Ensure success criteria apply across mediums	Provide instructors time to allow choice in the assignment they chose to redesign.
Integrate Multimodality a. Building towards multimodal assignments i. Understand which tools students have ii. Prompt students to reflect on multimodal skills iii. Empower students to create tech tutorials for peers iv. Help students become producers b. Supporting interaction with multimodal assignments i. Leverage video for robust discussions ii. Design collaborative multimodal assignments iii. Embed assignment overview videos iv. Provide audio/video feedback	Ask instructors to integrate multimodality. Instructors could choose to add multimodality to the assignment they are redoing, or they could choose to add surveys to better understand which tools students have access to in their courses.
Leverage Mobile-Friendly Tools a. Making use of the LMS a. Explore the LMS app and mobile-friendly recommendations b. Move assignments directly into the LMS c. Send students reminders to complete assignments b. Incorporating mobile-friendly tools to support active learning a. Use polling tools b. Support self-assessment with quizzing apps c. Provide a virtual space for formative peer–peer feedback d. Create your own QR codes e. Expand beyond the classroom with AR	Prompt instructors to move assignments as appropriate into the LMS or incorporate mobile-friendly tools like quizzing apps.
Wrap Up a. Looking forward: I've designed my mobile-friendly course … now what?	Ask instructors to reflect on their work today and set intentions for next steps. Instructors can reflect on the following questions:

(continued on next page)

Table 11.3 (Continued)

Agenda	*Activity Suggestions*
	1. What did you find most useful in designing mobile-friendly assignments? 2. What did you struggle with in creating a mobile-friendly assignment? 3. What will you implement in your courses today (or tomorrow) to make assignments more mobile-friendly? Give a brief preview of the next session on communicating to students the mobile-friendliness of courses.

Workshop #4: I've designed my mobile-friendly course … now what?

Mobile-friendly course design is a journey. After beginning to create more mobile-friendly course content and assignments, this interactive workshop will provide participants the space to answer the question "I've Designed My Mobile-Friendly Course … Now What?" Participants will first play and gain some first-hand experience using their mobile device to work through course content and complete assignments. Participants will then revisit the mobile-friendly course continuum to reevaluate the mobile-friendliness of their course. Finally, the session will conclude with participants creating a toolkit of mobile-friendly design lessons learned to share with colleagues in their department.

Goals

1. Play through reflection and iteration to build a better sense of the mobile experience of a course and revisions that can be adopted to make a course more mobile-friendly.

2. Adopt a method to communicate to students details on how they can make use of their mobile devices in our courses.
3. Create a toolkit of mobile-friendly course design lessons learned to share with colleagues in their department.

Model mobile use

When asking instructors to share their lessons learned on creating mobile-friendly courses in a toolkit, consider using a mobile-friendly tool like Padlet or Flip to curate advice or tips.

Make it local

Asking participants to create a toolkit of mobile-friendly course design lessons learned can help not only prompt reflections for workshop participants, but also inspire educators who were not able to attend the workshop. By asking participants to share their recommendations and experiences with colleagues in their department, we can create a localized toolkit that can help diffuse mobile-friendly course design approaches through a campus.

Workshop outline

Agenda	*Activity Suggestions*
Introduction a. Welcome b. Discuss goals c. Review agenda	If a tool has been used to facilitate communication between sessions, address frequently asked questions or interesting discussions to help frame this session.
Play! a. Playing through reflection i. View your course on a mobile device ii. Try out apps before you use them in class	Provide participants space to reflect on the student experience when using a phone to access course content and complete assignments. Ask participants to set intentions for playing through iteration. As a larger group, ask participants to share

(continued on next page)

Agenda	*Activity Suggestions*
iii. Survey students to generate a better understanding of their mobile experience iv. Test out aspects of your course students like to use a phone to complete b. Playing through iteration i. Make small changes to your course content to make it more mobile-friendly ii. Make small changes to your assignments to make them more mobile-friendly iii. Revise directions for students to make activities easier to complete on their phones iv. Empower students to share how they use mobile devices for courses	intentions to curate a list of ways in which courses can be iterated upon to become more mobile-friendly.
Communicate a. Communicating mobile-friendliness as an instructor i. Describe how students can use their phones for learning in the syllabus ii. Create a mobile-friendly syllabus iii. Send a welcome email to explain the mobile-friendliness of a course iv. Establish systems to indicate mobile-friendly assignments or course content v. Use mobile-friendly tools b. Communicating mobile-friendliness as an institution i. Develop educator learning communities on mobile-friendly course design ii. Build awareness of local student uses of mobile devices for learning iii. Showcase students who make use of phones for learning iv. Create mobile-friendly registration processes	Ask instructors to revisit the mobile-friendly course continuum and rank where their course falls on the continuum in terms of assignments and course content. Allow instructors to choose one of the strategies to communicate mobile-friendliness in their courses and provide space for instructors to begin to apply to a course.

(continued on next page)

Agenda	*Activity Suggestions*
v. Create an institution-wide system for communicating mobile-friendly courses vi. Ensure tools are mobile-friendly before committing to a site-wide license vii. Adopt mobile-friendly LMSs	
Wrap Up Look to the future	Ask instructors to reflect on how their course has become more mobile-friendly throughout these workshop sessions. Provide instructors their original evaluation on the mobile-friendly course continuum with the evaluation they completed in this session. Ask instructors to create a toolkit of mobile-friendly course design takeaways that can be shared with department colleagues.

The power of meaningful professional development

Creating mobile-friendly courses is a journey. Meaningful professional development helps to support educators as they embark and continue on the mobile-friendly course design journey. As educators, we are constantly reflecting and iterating on our teaching to better serve students. To fully implement mobile-friendly course design as an ongoing component of teaching practice, professional development needs to be active, reflective, and iterative. Educators need professional development on mobile-friendly course design that extends beyond a one-off workshop and fosters reflection.

The workshop outlines shared in this chapter provide a model for integrating reflective professional development in which educators actively apply mobile-design principles to their own course. By structuring the workshops as a series, educators have the opportunity to reflect and iterate on their course design over an extended period of time. The workshops help to foster a sense of growth. Educators are not expected to design a perfect mobile-friendly course by the end of the workshops, but instead, they are expected to show growth and progress along the mobile-friendly course continuum.

Facilitators of the workshops also have the opportunity to localize the workshops through the incorporation of data specific to their institution and attention to campus-specific instances of LMSs. Though the principles of mobile-design apply across institutions, integrating these principles in localized contexts can help educators to apply the principles in meaningful ways for their students and their departments.

Modeling mobile throughout the workshops also provides an opportunity for educators to gain a student's perspective of mobile-friendly tools. By modeling the use of mobile-friendly tools throughout these workshops, educators can develop an understanding of what it is like to use tools as a student. This invaluable perspective will not only help them support students when using similar tools in their classrooms, but also help to inspire adoption of mobile-friendly tools in their own teaching to support active learning.

As educators, we have a tremendous amount of responsibility. We are serving and guiding students as they pursue degrees and educational experiences that will not only change their lives, but also the lives of their families and community. Reducing barriers of access through the adoption of mobile-friendly course design can transform education for our students. These workshops provide an opportunity to offer meaningful professional development that supports educators on their mobile-design journey.

References

Darling-Hammond, L., Hyler, M. E., & Gardner, M. (2017). Effective Teacher Professional Development. Research Brief. *Learning Policy Institute.*

Mellow, G. O., Woolis, D. D., Klages-Bombich, M., & Restler, S. (2015). *Taking college teaching seriously-pedagogy matters!: Fostering student success through faculty-centered practice improvement.* Stylus Publishing, LLC.

12

LOOK TO THE FUTURE

REIMAGINING ACCESS TO HIGHER EDUCATION

Beginning with the past

My grandmother, Montine, had to stop going to school in fifth grade. She grew up on a farm in rural Arkansas, and when she turned ten, she was expected to stay home to help on the farm and in the kitchen. She would sometimes sneak into the barn to read, but her mom would quickly find her and punish her. Montine loved to read, but she wasn't supposed to with all the work on the farm. Montine desperately wanted to continue her education. For Montine, education was a way to a better life.

When she had her own family, she ensured all seven of her children graduated with a high school degree. This was no small feat as her life and the lives of her children were not easy. Her husband would often be gone for months at a time, and she would function as an only parent. They experienced homelessness and lived under a bridge for the summer when they first moved to Northern California. Instead of Christmas trees, my mom decorated tumbleweeds to get a feeling of Christmas. It was a

DOI: 10.4324/9781003328773-17

struggle to feed everyone, and hunger was no stranger to Montine and her children.

Montine and her husband worked as migrant farmers. One of my mom's earliest memories was Montine carrying her while picking cotton. When my mom got older, she would earn money to buy school clothes each year by working in the fields. As migrant workers, my mom's family moved frequently to follow the crops. By the time my mom graduated high school, she had attended about eight different schools. She went to schools across California – from the desert outside of Indio, to the coast near San Luis Obispo, to the fields outside of Bakersfield, to the valley in Northern California.

Montine saw education as a way to a better life for her children, and she passed this profound respect for education to my mom. When my mom was in high school, her science teacher told her to give up on going to college. Her science teacher told her that the best she could hope for would be to marry a rich farmer. My mom ignored this advice and enrolled in Sacramento City College. She lived in a small farming town about an hour away from the college and didn't have a car. The only way she could get to class was hitchhiking. She ate mostly only bananas as this was all she could afford. Ultimately, my mom wasn't able to persist in pursuing her degree, but, just like Montine, she passed a passion for education to me and did everything she could to make sure I was able to go further in my education than she did.

My mom taught me how to study and helped me develop routines to work on my homework when I got home from school. When I was in middle school, she told me that colleges would look at my grades (I still am not sure if she thought this was true or if she was just trying to get me to take middle school seriously). She listened to me practice my five-minute speech for Spanish class every night for a week even though she didn't understand a word I was saying. And when I was in college, she would call me and make sure I wasn't ever considering dropping out (I wasn't). During my credential program, she loaned me her car a few times a week so I could get to the school where I student taught – even though this meant she was without a car and about 45 minutes away from the grocery store. I was raised with stories of the power of education and the hope my grandmother had for what education could mean for her children's lives.

In my family, I've seen how the power of education transforms a generation's experience. My grandmother and her children had a difficult life. My mother was able to finish high school and take some college courses, and our lives were vastly different from how she grew up. My daughter has two parents with PhDs and wants to become a mathematician; her life is different even from how I grew up.

As educators, we are helping our students as they work to change not only their lives, but the lives of their families. To accomplish this vital and overwhelming task, we need to make use of all the tools that we have available. With near ubiquitous mobile device ownership (Pew Research Center, 2021), mobile devices provide a powerful tool to support learning anytime and anywhere. Although my mom wasn't able to complete her college degree, I sometimes imagine what her experience would be like if she was a student today. With the pervasiveness of mobile device ownership, it is likely that she would have some sort of mobile device. Although she may not have access to home internet or even a computer that was solely hers, she could have completed some readings and worked through some assignments on her phone. Although a mobile-friendly course wouldn't provide her the food or transportation she needed, it would provide her more flexibility and remove the extra hurdle of having to somehow get to the campus library to do all her coursework. By embarking on the mobile-friendly course design journey, we can help to support students as they seek education and a way toward a better life.

Serving all our students with an eye to the future

Mobile design allows us as educators to serve all our students and to support students as they seek the transformative power of education. Creating mobile-friendly courses offers us as educators a unique opportunity to both design for how students use their phones in their personal lives and to reduce barriers of access to education. Mobile-friendly course design is an approach to UDL that provides students equal access to a course regardless of which device they are using. Many of our students are accessing our courses on mobile devices, because:

- their phone is convenient,
- they don't have access to reliable home internet,

- they are working coursework into the in-between parts of their day,
- their phone is the newest technology they own, and/or
- they are experiencing temporary displacement or are experiencing homelessness.

The reality is our students are using phones to complete coursework (Robert, 2021). By creating mobile-friendly courses, we can maximize the benefits of mobile devices for learning and leverage the tools students are already using to make progress in their education.

Students experiencing homelessness

Creating mobile-friendly courses can help remove the stigma students experiencing homelessness may feel and create opportunities for students to interact without calling negative attention to students relying on their phone for learning. Students experiencing homelessness may be scared that their peers will discover they are currently homeless. As one student noted:

> Sometimes I feel like I can't be open about what I have gone through because I worry that I am going to be judged negatively forever. So, I lie about my access to certain things (internet, money to print, transportation) so I don't get singled out. It was hard to be homeless and figure out where to leave my stuff while I was on campus. When I had a safe place to leave belongings, I tried hard to appear as someone who was appropriately housed. My self-esteem was low, and I wanted to look like everyone else in my classes who were put together.
>
> (Sevieux, 2022)

For students experiencing homelessness, they want to be able to go to school and not be "singled out" as homeless.

Many students experiencing homelessness may have access to smartphones (Russell, 2019) and may rely on their phone for survival. Mobile-friendly courses have the potential to not only make our courses accessible to students experiencing homelessness, but also have the potential for students to build meaningful connections with their instructors and peers. There is no doubt there is a stigma to homelessness, and students experiencing homelessness can suffer from extreme loneliness (Rokach, 2005; Rokach, 2014). But for students experiencing homelessness, education can be a way out of poverty (Beckett, 2022), and the desire for education is urgent.

Imagine if a course was fully mobile-friendly and a student could complete the entire course with their phone. For a student experiencing homelessness, this means that they could continue to make progress toward their education, and they could use the tools to which they have access. The stigma of their technology would be removed, and they wouldn't have to feel bad for only having a phone to complete coursework. In fact, imagine if the phone was used to facilitate discussions via mobile-friendly backchannels. By providing these opportunities for students to interact, we could eliminate students' concerns about their current state of homelessness being discovered by their peers. They could interact freely in these mobile-friendly discussions and build meaningful connections without revealing their appearance or hygiene. For youth experiencing homelessness, building connections via mobile devices has the potential to support not only learning, but also mental health (Rice et al., 2011).

Students who are parents

Mobile-friendly course design also has the potential to serve students who are parents. We know the myth of the so-called 18- to 22-year-old college student who has no children and only has to focus on school is no longer the norm. In fact, about one-fifth of undergraduates are parents (Huerta et al., 2021). For students who are parents, obtaining an education holds tremendous power. A degree can mean health care, better work hours, more flexibility, and a living wage. More importantly, these parents will be able to give their children a good life with food on the table and visits to the doctor when needed. But balancing parenthood with college is no small feat. As one mother of three noted, "It's like, how do you say, like a juggler. You have to try to juggle school, work, the kids, a little alone time, a lot of study time, a lot of homework time" (Huerta et al., 2021, p. 1). Students who are parents face tremendous time constraints as they balance childcare and academic responsibilities (Reed et al., 2021).

For these students, it can be difficult (if not impossible) to find uninterrupted extended chunks of time to complete coursework. As one student noted, "I don't have time for me, and for my daughter. It's just, I mean, it's a few hours. So, if I am not sleeping or eating, I am studying" (Huerta et al., 2021). Mobile-friendly courses that are designed to be completed in ten-minute or shorter chunks can have a profound impact for students who are also caring for children. In these cases, students can effectively make use of the in-between parts of their day, while waiting to pick their kids up from school, nursing their child at 3:00 a.m., or watching their children play at the park. Students who are parents may feel a pull between making progress toward their degree and being present with their children. Mobile-friendly courses make use of the in-between parts of the day, so students don't have to choose between their kids and completing their own coursework.

Another barrier for students who are parents is access to the tools needed to be successful in college: internet, computers, and transportation. As one community college parent noted, "I can't afford Internet. So that's another challenge for me. I try to work with what I have" (Huerta et al., 2021). These students may also spend a good portion of time on public transportation taking their kids to school and going to their own campus (Huerta et al., 2021). In these cases, mobile-friendly courses provide the opportunity to access their courses without home internet and make use of time on public transportation for learning. By designing courses that effectively leverage the potential of mobile devices for anytime/anywhere learning (Ally, 2013; Barden & Bygroves, 2018), we can support students who are parents as they seek degrees to improve their lives and the lives of their children.

Students working full-time

Mobile-friendly courses also help us serve students who are working full-time. The long-lasting impacts of the COVID-19 pandemic and its impacts on the economy have had profound implications for those making a choice between going to college and getting a full-time job. With "unprecedented wage growth" in the service industry and strong demand after the initial hard closures due to the pandemic (Moran, 2021), many students found themselves wondering why a college degree would be useful when they could make so much money working full-time without a degree. However, those who decide to work full-time may find themselves wanting to pursue a degree as their families grow and their income does not keep pace with their growing needs. For these learners, mobile design helps to transform a choice between school and work. It creates high-quality educational opportunities that break down the dichotomy between school and work and offers access to students who need to work while they learn.

Mobile-friendly courses can help us also serve students who are working full-time but are seeking to gain new skills to remain competitive in a rapidly changing workforce. As educators, we are increasingly preparing students for emerging careers. In fact, a majority of students entering elementary school will ultimately have jobs that don't yet exist (Schwab & Samans, 2016). As educators, we will increasingly need to serve learners who need to reskill and/or upskill while they are working full-time (Li, 2022).

Reskilling requires someone to learn an entirely new skill (Li, 2022) and is essential for those in the workforce who are facing the loss of jobs. As more and more jobs become automated, we will need to be able to help those whose industry has evaporated through reskilling. Upskilling allows someone to learn a new skill that is related to their current industry, and with rapidly emerging technologies, this will be increasingly important. For example, as artificial intelligence (AI) becomes more pervasive and infused into our daily lives, the workforce will need to be able to quickly adapt and develop new skills to effectively use AI in their work. To best serve learners in a rapidly changing workforce, we need to create flexible learning experiences that fit into learners' lives. Workers will need to be able to have increased access to educational opportunities as they will likely be wanting to reskill or upskill while they balance full-time jobs. As such, mobile design provides a powerful opportunity to meet the needs of anytime/anywhere learning, convenience, and flexibility that will be essential to those navigating the future of jobs.

Serving all students through flexibility

As we look to the future, one key feature emerges: learners will increasingly need flexibility. Learners need courses that fit into their lives instead of trying to fit their lives into a course. With increasing income inequality (Pew Research Center, 2020), reducing barriers of access to high-quality educational opportunities is more important than ever. Designing mobile-friendly courses can help students experiencing homelessness both continue to persist in their degree and connect with other students in their courses. Mobile design also serves students who are parents who are seeking to better their lives and the lives of their families through education. We can also leverage mobile design to serve those who are working full-time as well as those who are navigating the future of jobs (Li, 2022). When one person in a community gets a degree it not only changes their lives, but the lives of everyone around them. As educators, embarking on the mobile-friendly course design journey can help us to meet the needs of students today who need flexibility as they experience homelessness, care for young children, or work full-time jobs. It also helps us to meet the needs of our future students who are just now in elementary school and will one day have jobs we didn't even know existed.

Serving our community by transcending classrooms and laptop screens

A journey begins with one step. Mobile design is a journey. Our courses will not become mobile-friendly overnight. But step by step, we can create courses that leverage the powerful technology students carry with them in their pockets. As we embark on this journey, we also need to have an eye to where we're headed. Education holds tremendous potential to transform the lives of individuals, but it is also foundational to our ability as a society to address the existential threat of climate change as well as to continue to function as a democracy. Across the globe, we are facing profound challenges that can only be faced with education and innovation. These challenges include the following:

- shrinking middle class,
- increasing number of households living in poverty,
- hungry children,
- people experiencing homelessness,
- polarization, and
- climate change.

As educators, we carry a heavy load. We are in the business of changing people's lives and making dreams come true. We are also uniquely positioned to help society address the challenges ahead through education. Education can raise individuals, families, and communities out of poverty. Education can help to reduce polarization by helping individuals question false news and by helping communities who are facing disappearing economies reskill and find new jobs. Education can not only help communities make the necessary changes to reduce the impacts of climate change, but also spur the innovation that will be necessary to navigate a changing climate.

More people than ever have access to powerful technologies that reduce barriers of access to education. We cannot face the challenges ahead of us in the next 50 years without the power of education. A lot has changed since my grandmother was a little girl and wasn't allowed to continue in school, but education still has the power to change lives. Whether we are facing climate change or poverty, education is the first and arguably most crucial step toward addressing these existential threats. With mobile design, we can create courses that transcend the walls of a classroom or the screen of a laptop to help learners face today's challenges as well as the challenges of tomorrow.

References

Ally, M. (2013). Mobile learning: From research to practice to impact education. *Learning and Teaching in Higher Education: Gulf Perspectives*, 10(2), 3–12.

Barden, O., & Bygroves, M. (2018). 'I wouldn't be able to graduate if it wasn't for my mobile phone.' The affordances of mobile devices in the construction of complex academic texts. *Innovations in Education and Teaching International*, 55(5), 555–565. 10.1080/14703297.2017.1322996

Beckett, L. (2022). 'My car is my home': The California students with nowhere to live. *The Guardian*. https://www.theguardian.com/us-news/2022/apr/02/college-students-unhoused-school-help#:~:text=A%202020%20survey%20of%20195%2C000,surfing%E2%80%9D%20or%20staying%20with%20friends

Huerta, A.H., Rios-Aguilar, C., Ramirez, D., & Muñoz, M. (2021). Like a juggler: The experiences of racially minoritized student parents in a

California Community College. *UC Davis Wheelhouse*. https://education.ucdavis.edu/sites/main/files/wheelhouse_research_brief_vol_6_no_3_final.pdf

Li, L. (2022). Reskilling and upskilling the future-ready workforce for industry 4.0 and beyond. *Information Systems Frontiers*, 1–16.

Moran, A. (2021). An industry's comeback: Service and hospitality jobs see unprecedented wage growth. *Washington Post Jobs*. https://jobs.washingtonpost.com/article/an-industry-s-comeback-service-and-hospitality-jobs-see-unprecedented-wage-growth/

Pew Research Center (2020). Trends in income and wealth inequality. https://www.pewresearch.org/social-trends/2020/01/09/trends-in-income-and-wealth-inequality/

Pew Research Center (2021). Mobile fact sheet. https://www.pewresearch.org/internet/fact-sheet/mobile/

Reed, S., Grosz, M., Kurlaender, M., and Cooper, S. (2021). A portrait of student parents in the California Community Colleges. *UC Davis Wheelhouse*. https://education.ucdavis.edu/sites/main/files/wheelhouse_research_brief_vol_6_no_2_v2.pdf

Rice, E., Lee, A., & Taitt, S. (2011). Cell phone use among homeless youth: Potential for new health interventions and research. *Journal of Urban Health*, *88*(6), 1175–1182. 10.1007/s11524-011-9624-z

Robert, J. (2021). EDUCAUSE QuickPoll results: Flexibility and equity for student success. *EDUCAUSE Review*. https://er.educause.edu/articles/2021/11/educause-quickpoll-results-flexibility-and-equity-for-student-success

Rokach, A. (2005). Private lives in public places: Loneliness of the homeless. *Social Indicators Research*, *72*(1), 99–114.

Rokach, A. (2014). Loneliness of the marginalized. *Open Journal of Depression*, *3*, 147–153. 10.4236/ojd.2014.34018

Russell, M. (2019). Smartphones are a lifeline for the young homeless. If only they had Wi-Fi. San Francisco Chronicle. https://www.sfchronicle.com/business/article/Smartphones-are-a-lifeline-for-the-young-13582809.php

Schwab, K., & Samans, R. (2016). The future of jobs: Employment, skills and workforce strategy for the fourth industrial revolution. *World Economic Forum*. http://hdl.voced.edu.au/10707/393272

Sevieux, J. (2022). How BC students experiencing homelessness get it done. *BC Academic Tech Blog*. https://bcacademictechnology.wordpress.com/2022/09/01/how-bc-students-experiencing-homelessness-get-it-done/

INDEX

Note: *Italicized*, **bold** and ***bold italics*** refer to figures, tables and boxes.